HE KÁRMÁN LINE   DAISY ATTERBURY

contents

$$L = \tfrac{1}{2}\, \rho V^2\, SC_L$$

Stars arrive non-visually, first.
—Mei-mei Berssenbrugge

A blue orbit suggested by echoes.
—Tommy Pico

Below this line, space belongs to each country.
Above this level there would be free space.
—Theodore von Kármán

places (in no particular order).

Santa Fe Plaza
Ensisheim, Alsace
Alsace–Lorraine
Glorieta Mountain
White Sands Missile Range
Truth or Consequences
Spaceport America
Cottonwood Mall
Belt of Venus
Brooklyn
Jiffy Lube
Charon
Los Alamos National Labs
The Very Large Array
Zone of Avoidance
Solar Observatory
European Space Agency
Jornada del Muerto
Templum Pacis of Rome
Institute of the Cosmos
Azores archipelago
Albuquerque
Sushi King
Trinity Site
Fifth Avenue
Riga
Near Space
Meteorite Museum
Manhattan
Santa Maria
Waste Isolation Pilot Project

Your Secret Swimming Pool
The Poetry Project
Primo Auto Parts
New Mexico Route 599
Earth's Moon
E Train
Mojave Desert
Tinder
Queens
Mars (Simulation)
Liwa Oasis

after star death.

The Kármán Line

They say, *No love deserves the death it has.* Fuck! I see about the loss of you before we even begin. I've never been satisfied with the imagined end. She said, *This class discussion is the best so far. However sex is an*

> *inhibiting topic*

> what it means
> to deplane

The Kármán line is the altitude at which the Earth's atmosphere ends and outer space begins. The Kármán line is the edge of space, as opposed to near space, the *high altitude* region of the atmosphere. When they say *altitude* they're thinking in terms of the human. What is measurable from the ground. Beyond the Kármán line the Earth's atmosphere is too thin to support an object in flight.

A plane at that height would have to travel faster than orbital velocity to remain in the air. Space begins as determined by math and the practicality of actually being somewhere.

Because of the difficulty in determining the exact point at which the boundary occurs, there is still no legal definition of the line between a country's air space and outer space. Below the Kármán line space belongs to each country directly below it. Above the Kármán line, space is considered *free*. One hundred kilometers is an accepted boundary between earth and space for many purposes.

I imagine a few purposes

I have my own lunch hour

Knowledge of space can be a nonreciprocal relationship. *Known* means something enters into a relationship with something or someone else—even if the recipient, the known, does not enter into the relationship with something like willingness. Even if the recipient, the known, whether person or thing is unaware, does not know. I know the taste of grammar in my mouth.

lack

address

And space is populated and unknown.

A compilation of notes composed in the year and a half before his death, Wittgenstein's *On Certainty* is an incomplete and imprecise documentation of his operation upon epistemological longing. The notes detail exemptions to doubt, the default, dominant mode of rhetorical arbitration. *On Certainty* is about belief, which is the Kármán line.

661. How might I be mistaken in my assumption that I was never on the moon?

662. If I were to say "I have never been on the moon—but I may be mistaken," that would be idiotic

And yet I want to say, I have never been on the moon

In all certainty, I

Leave my knowing

To unreasonable doubt

L = ½ $\rho V^2 SC_L$
where L is
the lift force

ρ
air density
v
the aircraft's speed
relative to air

S is
the aircraft's wing area
CL the
lift coefficient
point
blank

I was once *I'm here*

at the surface

Out of order

poets do it

this imperial poesy

　　　point at it:

　　　its killing mesh

Word being both

administration

against memory

and the means

At first it's an inch

then it's a couple inches

then it's a couple feet

She will reach the Kármán line[1]

it's lonely up here

at the shell of the Earth

and cold

Zones of Avoidance

I read the headline that astronomers have recently discovered a vast assemblage of galaxies hidden behind our own in what they call the "Zone of Avoidance."

I ignore an astronomer who super-likes me on Tinder. *Beyond the Milky Way a Galactic Wall.* I wonder if she's picked up that I love stars in a moody, non-scientific way. I wonder if I'm scared someone will reduce my life to math, if I fear I'll meet my match and we'll exist in the world computationally-compositionally. *There is a vast wall across the southern border of the local cosmos.* I do in fact want to know about this with my body.

The thousands of new galaxies are described in the *New York Times* using Earth metaphors like *beehives of trillions of stars and dark worlds* and *a curtain arcing across at least 700 million light-years of space.* I press my hands to my eyes the better to see bees bursting, exploding bees taking a bow, the man behind the curtain naked in genderless stardust drapes. Is the language of science a zone of contagion, where metaphor bleeds into metaphor, because reality is so far outside the language we've reserved for it, we almost glitch?

I attach some sanctity of thinking to our exchanges, because *I think* you've taught me how to think. I've aligned thinking with some excruciating ecstasy of relation possible only though this exchange and thus confined to it, a thinking provoked and then possessed by another *in service of a togetherness.* When my possession ends there is another form it takes *I think*, which is thinking corroded by pain and loss. It's probably that thought, as narrative, produces some chemical release that has me doubled over the toilet seeing stars.

People talk about radical softness. Hard elements become the catastrophic aftermath of the merger of dense cores of stars left after star death. The Mohs hardness scale's gradation ranges from talc to diamond, the between occupied by gems like topaz, apatite, and fluorite. Hydrogen, helium, and lithium, the universe's three lightest elements, were created earliest in the birth of the cosmos, while heavier elements were forged billions of years later in the dense cores of stars.

I try to describe contact past my galaxy's Zone of Avoidance, the place I find myself with nothing to lose and every bone in my body healed like a hardened jewel.

Je bâtis a roches mon langage[2]
I build my language with rocks

Hardness is a spectrum. I linger with the idea of an aesthetics of gleaming. Which is not to say *not* chaos. It's a place where thought is disorder. Where there are fresh sheets.

Some larger majority of the investigations go unanswered, someone writes in the app. **instigations,* she corrects. I don't think I answer.

Everyday Silver

In the back of her pickup I think, *I'll burn my ass here to make something happen.* Nothing happens. I'm in the truck she bought on Craigslist. She plans to resell the truck for more money in Florida.

I read aloud about the space boom coming to our local economy. There's a website tagline for Spaceport America. *Imagine sitting in the cockpit of a space vehicle and launching from a two-mile-long runway in the middle of a New Mexico desert. Imagine the heart-pounding, dizzying effect of weightlessness in outer space.* Imagine all of this.

Not for me, she says, picking at a piece of rubber in the truck bed.

No?

You'd have come with me. You like all the money and fuss.

Spaceport America is an active test facility and is closed to public access. Launches at the site are not open to public viewing and are subject to scheduling changes. Private tours of the facilities can be arranged in advance through our tour provider Final Frontier Tours.

My sticky thighs make loud tacky sounds on the truck.

To you, I'd say, Spaceport America's theme song is country.

To me, you'd say no, it's the whole of Taylor Swift discography playing at once.

Space, really, is a giant Rorschach. Into it we send rockets and satellites and space stations. But more than that, we send beliefs.

Instead, I ask about her plans for Florida.

Spaceport America has a food truck.
Spaceport America has an open bar.
Spaceport America has hi-speed Wi-Fi.
Spaceport America has vials of your DNA.

There's a Mars simulation in Nevada. Another recently
closed in Hawaii. You applied to Mars and were *selected*.
Imagine the luck of being plucked out of your life. Imagine
living on a planet no one can reach. Not Spectrum robocalls,
not your boss, not your other ex. Sorry, but there are no
telephones on Mars.

Sorry you tell me, but there's no way to meet for coffee. Sorry,
sorry, sorry!

Truck bed scalding in the sun, I tell this story:

Long ago, my family participated in the Pet Parade in the
Fiestas de Santa Fe, a celebration of bloody reconquest of
New Mexico by Spanish conquistadors in the 1600s. Since
I've grown up, there's been grudging acknowledgment here
that this celebration sits in a square wrongness. Still, this
acknowledgement is contested. Counterstories have been
fought for, bled for, for centuries.

Memory allows me to describe this scene:

My dad, mom, two sisters, and myself in alien costumes
pulling a guinea pig cage decorated up like the Mars Rover.

Hello there, this series is a meditation on limits.

Hi back, I'm here to translate an encounter.

Words in an app

Old stories, a long history
      of getting yours

Cosmic Bulletin

According to the European Space Agency, the island Santa Maria of the Azores archipelago may be the perfect site for an international spaceport. This is because of the clear stretches of ocean to the north and south. Santa Maria was colonized by Portuguese settlers beginning around 1443. Columbus sailed there in 1493. The European Space Agency finds Santa Maria beneficially close to Europe *for shipping purposes.*

Truth or Consequences, New Mexico, is considered an ideal location for Spaceport America, because of its proximity to White Sands Missile Range, a US Army firing range in southern New Mexico. The area became a name on a map on July 9, 1945, days before the first-ever nuclear weapon was detonated at the at the northern part of the range, the Trinity Site. The largest military installation in the States, White Sands Missile Range is the perfect site to share airspace with a commercial spaceport. Launch complexes have been built for US missile tests Nike Hercules and Nike Zeus, which are now coordinated around launches for space missions by SpaceX and Virgin Galactic.

Space, enough absence, is at a premium and must be cleared to be filled.

Things you might need to ship to a spaceport include things from land: food supplies, industrial materials, missiles, satellites. Things you might need to ship from a spaceport include things from space: metals, samples, (hopefully) water.

Dear _____, I felt you were speaking to me before I was born

Dear _____, I've imbued your output with meaning

Dear _____, There's some central misalignment

Dear _____, I've made myself your asteroid

A Orbex acaba de vencer um prémio (tal como a Lockeed Martin) para desenvolver um foguetão neste caso o Prime, no contexto da criação de um porto especial na Escócia, refere um comunicado.

I submit my writing on space to a journal called *Cosmic Bulletin*, run by the newly formed Institute of the Cosmos. The journal has been created for a biennial in Latvia which has since been delayed. I decide this is the right venue for my writings, a speculative project that has since been delayed.

I read about Tomás Saraceno, an Argentinian and Italian artist who is planning to fly his sculpture from Berlin to Riga powered only by air, sun, and wind in order to avoid shipping and thereby adding to the total of human-produced carbon emissions in the atmosphere. He asks, *What if a sculpture could carry itself to Riga?*

There's no telling when this exhibition will actually happen. After World War II, V-2 rockets were secretly shipped to the White Sands Missile Range in New Mexico, where they were disassembled and reassembled with the help of Wernher von Braun, the man who had developed them under Nazi Germany.

Twenty years after von Braun was making rockets for Hitler to bomb London, he was overseeing the American space program, building the Saturn V rocket that would fly us to the moon.

I separate thoughts about the commercial art world from an emotional response to a thing of beauty. Maybe separation points to faulty containers. I'm unsure how to reconcile *flow*, Moten and Harney, and *suspense*, my own fantasy of a life-way that buys time, then transcends it. I watch the artist Alejandro Cesarco's video of hands shuffling through faded color photographs of people in landscapes. Or I finger the casings of Barb Smith's tiny clay bells strung up without tongues. There's a sound absence makes, and it's the sound of shuffling, shuffling, shuffling. *Because my presence came to Earth as clandestine, it has always remained alive as absence, much like resonance from structureless bells.*

Meanwhile, we structure social norms around a dislike for seeing someone other than in their place. We fear the sudden wind of a betrayal of position, the ways it blows up our skirts and exposes the truth that we all have choices to make. What's new is language for what we're missing. What's old is a collective exhaustion of self-soothing, the feeling of drinking coffee and walking to the other side of "room" vaguely worried, not knowing what you are looking for.

My friend and I have a project called *Alien Monologues.* We write in a shared document mostly of longing and our confusion about the role of art in our lives, a project that demonstrates our commitment to potential over realization. For many months, my only contribution is to highlight all the text and turn it pink. Eventually, my friend writes, *It's like all the strings holding me down have been cut, and I'm floating through space. I don't want to be floating through space. I want a home.*

There's country music, one true line in one true song

This dangling thread threatening a fray
or a whole dynasty

Baby your song

You can't rely on
structure these folded
matchbooks I take one
greased packet of fire sauce
This makes a very large
salsa verde, ten calories

The way you discovered
money, you pissed me off
when we touched, I sort of
peeled back, a paint strip falling
from the pole. But we keep
contact. I muscle myself
into a tight shirt, press my face
against a glass pane, make notes

Towards future health
wondering if the problem is lack
of calories or ritual
lack. Dry as a bone
and full of vacancies

The cost of a cold beer near a lot, let's see, the cost is
stupid, is what it is. Millennial decay, my face
starting to reflect the landscape
I take on a cinderblock aesthetic
mostly behind the eyes
we're burning more cortisol
for the same tank

In space there's a Tiny House
isn't there, not a bill someone forgot
it hits home, this place you call
space, the last place I forgot
you can scratch the lotto
win nothing but your neighbor
Sunday said he tried last week
a kind of formal feeling
saturated sweet

Binary Asteroids

At the start of 2017, a binary asteroid is discovered approaching the Earth. Its eventual proximity to orbit classifies it as a near-Earth object. The asteroid is actually two bodies, one rotating around the other. The orbiting body is likely tidally locked to the primary body, which means it always has the same face toward its primary object. Usually only the orbiting object tidally locks to the larger body but in extreme cases, such as if the difference in mass and the distance between the objects is small, each object may be tidally locked to the other.

I go by myself to the Meteorite Museum in Albuquerque. Perhaps I'm preparing to write you. Perhaps I'm escaping this feeling of being utterly disconnected. If you were here I'd walk us to Glorieta Mountain where an iron pallasite meteorite from Mars was found in 1884. Or hike the Sandia Foothills where an iron meteorite was found in 1925. Or take you to the cases of meteorites, where I'm snapping pics and minding my business.

Perhaps like people in my life, these stones can be classified as falls or finds: falls, seen falling to the Earth and then collected; finds, chance discovery with no record of a fall. In 1492, a large stone meteorite fell near Ensisheim, Alsace, one of the first known recorded falls. In 1895, my grandfather's family left Alsace–Lorraine after it was annexed from France by Germany. When my family was forced to enlist in the German army, they fled to the United States.

The museum is black felt walls and booths and scotch-tape-like displays of real meteorites. The cases are dusty and labeled with bites of information on foam board printouts. The museum, I learn, is sponsored by the geology department and monitored by PhD students. These two are bunched behind a monitor, reminding me of myself, of you, of anyone with time to kill, scrolling, tapping, not talking.

Hey, I say, glancing at the table tent with visiting hours. MWF 11:00 AM – 5:00 PM.

Hi, they say, neither really looking up. The room's fluorescent lighting makes us all look too old to be dressing like this motley threesome in a back room off a hallway, museum.

I'm just going to look around.

I recall going to dinosaur museums as a kid. I picture an asteroid falling on circling mega-birds in Arizona, wonder if time would have been more real to me if I'd seen ancient creatures on display in their feathery, fleshy forms, not the big chalky bones kids memorized as exemplary of this other time, the dinosaur past. I used to think of history as always already dead.

In their almost DIY display cases, the meteorites look glitteringly alive. I come away with an impression of material—metal, like shiny iron with shallow depressions like thumbprints, or chondrites speckled with stony granules. New Mexico is a good place to find meteorites because so much of this land is desert. Only a handful of meteorites have been seen falling here, but hundreds have been found in dry lakebeds or desertified fields.

Preparing to convey all this and get on my way, I write an email in my head. I'm hoping to conjure what I need and yet the thing evades me. I've avoided this or it's avoided me all my life. I often find myself pulverized by abstract visions of the world's lack or my own.

I think about sneaking a drink in the bathroom as a kid. I think of slipping into a plaid sleeve from Ross in early body knowledge. I remember sneaking off when I should have been doing homework or waiting, calling my friends or comforting the person who asked. I still sneak off when I should be meditating or doing yoga. I can't own up to being like constrained people who have secret affairs in letters because I don't have letters, affairs, hope. I think I've been waiting until my condition, this body in space, will pass. Most of my writing is between arrivals, for example an email draft I write to myself: *Hello, it was good to receive your abject message. I'm doing fine and my address is* _____. I'm longing after upper body strength and defined musculature and halfheartedly doing one pushup.

I decide you route out all other falls, yourself a compelling find. I've seen how your manners outside my likes and preferences betray my desire to fix you in space. You're there on the page, that smell, your jacket, that taste, my spit. Then you're not, you're just this far, a phenomenon I can only describe as interpersonal remoteness. I begin these letters in my head.

> I map out simple spatial puzzles
> How many ways one zipper

> Clears the room

> *P.S.: more than anything please don't believe that it's*

*your absence I love, or rather my own love of your
absence...*[3]

On the bulletin next to a glass museum case dirty with
fingerprints, I read, *Craters give clues into a mass's history.* There's
a von Kármán crater on Mars. And I think from your bunker
on Mars, Nevada, you'd call these clues cosmic mark-making.

Spinoza thought pleasure was a bothersome craving like the
need for acclaim, something we require in small doses so we
don't go mad with want. I wonder, can I qualify this thing,
call it one word, *queer,* or others, meteoric, burning up on
contact, or cratering a hole, binary asteroids approaching
the Earth? And if I temporalize it, call it ancient, call it
history, call it pre-historic, pre-human, can I justify its total
integration? I find myself surrendering to a feeling.

In the earliest scientific theories of craters in the moon,
impacts were thought to have been created by gas bubbles
that rose up and blasted through the moon's surface, a
different form of contact. Now, we understand craters to
be measurements of trauma from transiting and colliding
objects. Here, in a manual, it says *participant injury.* Here,
it says *payload.* This manual is for transiting and colliding
humans. Whereas, I can point to the parts of my body that
already know what *participant injury* means, what connects me
to space and sex and harm. I can say dislocate. By which
I may not mean disassociate.

A meteorite is of the Earth because it lands, however remote
its origins. Its proximities to its primary body are not up
for debate, the way I wish to see a person in the morning.
An asteroid is of space and is matter outside the matter we

know, the way I picture you at a near-total remove. If I write *you're open* and you write *you open me*, there's something sweet. You've named what I wish this were, not letters alighting my retinae, but the parting folds of skin.

Pluto and its moon Charon are tidally locked, so close in proximity and mass. They face each other's face. But this is not true of Pluto's other moons, Styx, Nix, Kerberos, and Hydra. These are said to rotate chaotically.

In *My Meteorite*, Harry Dodge writes, *The procedure to check if an iron meteorite is real, that is, whether the body of the material was formed in space and not terrestrially, is to slice off a piece and check the guts of the thing.* I've made notes, of iron guts and slicings. There's the truth that a surface can become an opening. Then, there's the truth that I have no sense of your tidal proclivities, your whereabouts, or whether you're ever coming back.

I wish to actually sit and locate my body in space. I can admit I'm utterly lonely for want of the good food. I can see that the problem of never getting touched is a total infrastructural problem. I can take my position as more than a problem of feeling, but not superior to a problem of feeling. Knowing all this, I still put down my throw rug and made coffee. I stare at the wall in trance or I touch myself to arrive back to my body, this place, and you.

I take a brochure. This will get me through the next few days. I leave the museum through the hallway I entered, wave goodbye to nonresponsive PhDs, and exit to a white summer day.

Dear workers of the Earth, it's not working. It's these oversized

EXxxxxxCAVATIONS

I see lumpy bumpy surfaces of cooled dust

A sign on the bathroom

Out of order

I gave up the sauce

Drank cream

exosphere.

thermosphere.

mesosphere.

stratosphere.

troposphere.

Mars Simulation Application

1. Please write your name. Include the following: Surname/ Family name, Given name, Title (optional). What would you like to be called by your crewmates (if not your given name)?

2. Please write your postal address complete with postal code and country and denote whether the address is: Home, Work, School, or Other (please specify)

3. Do you have US citizenship, permanent resident status, a US visa that will remain in force through June 2021, or will you acquire a tourist or other visa in order to visit?

4. Please list the email address you want to use for all correspondence from the Mars Society (one only).

5. Please enter the dates of the rotations (listed below) that you are available to serve on a _____ crew.

NOTE: Select as many rotations as you possibly can; the more flexible you can be, the higher your chances of being placed on a team and/or getting your preferred rotation. In addition, we also welcome applications for one-week, three-week, or four-week rotations. Please indicate if you would like an alternative rotation length and the dates you wo uld like us to consider.

(Please note that all rotations begin with arrival at _____ on Saturday morning and end with departure on Sunday morning. All crews are required to spend one overlapping day with the new crew for handover. No exceptions.)

6. If you have served on a space analog crew or long-term expedition crew in the past, please list your experience. Specify the facility or location, the duration of your mission, the number of crewmembers serving with you, and your role in the mission.

7. For safety reasons, _____ crew members must be physically fit enough to perform outdoor work in cold and/or hot conditions wearing heavy mock space suits. They must have sufficient fine motor skill for typical handwriting and typing tasks, and sufficient (corrected) visual and hearing acuity for independent (non-assisted) participation in all aspects of the crew's work and communications. Please choose one of the responses—if you choose the second, and are otherwise qualified to join a crew, we may contact you to answer your questions and discuss your situation.

8. _____ is located at least 45 minutes from the nearest emergency medical service and about 2.5 hours from the nearest full-service hospital. If you have a major health condition that could impact your stay at _____ (e.g. diabetes, asthma, high blood pressure, cancer, cardiovascular disease, blood clots, mental illness, autoimmune disease, major allergies, or substance abuse issues), or have a history of any of these health conditions including heart attack or stroke, we may ask you to obtain clearance from your physician before participating at _____ and to discuss your situation privately with us before accepting you to a crew.

9. Crews at _____ live in close physical proximity to each

other. If you carry a communicable disease which can be passed from person to person in a normal living environment (e.g. tuberculosis, Hepatitis C) we expect you to discuss your situation with your doctor and disclose it with us. If you select the second option, and are otherwise qualified to join a crew, we will contact you.

Read over the skill sets for the crew positions in a typical _____ crew in the instructions that accompany this application and decide which ones are best suited to your skills, experience, and interests. Roles include Commander, Executive Officer, Health and Safety Officer, Crew Engineer, GreenHab Officer, Crew Geologist, Crew Biologist, Crew Astronomer, Crew Scientist, and Crew Journalist/Artist/Communicator/Media Officer. If you are applying as a professional Artist-in-Residence, please indicate this. Professionals may indicate their preference for a crew role other than those listed above. However, it is the responsibility of the applicant to provide evidence that they are qualified for this role and also that a significant part of their work at _____ will reflect this role. It is at the discretion of the Crew Selection Committee to grant titles other than those listed.

Member of The Mars Society or affiliates (e.g. Mars Society Australia, etc.)

Prior _____ or _____ crewmember

Prior member of other analog facility expedition (e.g. _____, _____, _____, etc.)

Member of a team whose home institution/group has a multi-year history of successful participation at _____

Analog astronaut (simulation)

Mars Analog research (no simulation)

Medical Training (e.g. First aid, First responder, EMT, nurse, M.D.)

Greenhouse management

Field research (Geology/Geophysics, Biology, Meteorology, etc.)

Lab research (Chemistry, Biology, Physics, Horticulture, etc.)

Living off-grid

Living/working in wilderness/remote setting

Working in extreme environments

Leadership

Group participation showing a long-term commitment, for example, clubs that you have participated as an active member over a period of time (does not have to be Mars/space related)

Home repair and maintenance (e.g. plumbing, carpentry, electrical, heating/cooling, propane, and water pumps)

Mechanical skills (e.g. engine repair and maintenance)

Electronic skills (e.g. soldering, measurement, testing, troubleshooting and repair)

IT skills (e.g. operation, configuration and connectivity of computers, Wi-fi, networked devices, basic network commands)

Communications (e.g. ham radio operator, repeater operations)

Aviation experience, including drones

Cooking

Traveling by ATV and/or 4WD

GPS and map reading

Expedition management

Social media

Multi-lingual

Communication and collaboration with diverse cultural groups not centrally located

Maintenance and cleaning of a research facility

Maintenance and cleaning of a communal living facility

Graduate education

Specialized training related to analog research

Relevant licenses/certificates held

Prior published research on Mars analog research
Any other skills you feel are relevant to being a crewmember
at _____   *Yes*

The Searchers

Have you been in an airport, thirsty pondering the scarcity of *clean water on this Earth*?

Me   Describe a lunar mission in 5 words or less, in 2 words or less, in 1 word or less

You   Describe an orbital body in 5 words or less, in 2 words or less, in 1 word or less

rice_cube   Do you skip the 13th flight like good hotels have no 13th floor?

I know the kind of problem that arises. I like to be in touch in different ways. I can hope to remain at least somewhat open to my undoing. If it means continuing to love when you're dissenting, which is choosing, I agree. I undo myself in order to be together. Until I can no longer feel a thing.

I used to take the G train to the E train to the Q64 bus to work, thinking about my friend having *unsuccessful sex* and saying it's *love*. What was unsuccessful? Giving up on some tired idea of electric touch, I agreed, like I never knew life with its monetizing sugar. Or never saw a vegetable in my whole life.

I am thinking about language and intimacy listening to Nathaniel Mackey. I write down, *Where words went made soul matter*. I think about you lending me a book, all that language. We're down to Earth now, we're on the floor, piloting new theories of reading. We're outside, we're on the bus, in temporary housing. We're flipping pages, changing clothes. We changed tense. It's not just that words made soul matter, but it's where they *went* that did. And he is talking about the soul *mattering* but also the *stuff* of soul, its *matter.*

Some say the soul is mixed in with the whole universe, and perhaps this is why Thales supposed that all things are full of gods. From what is related about him, it seems that Thales too held that the soul is something productive of motion, if indeed he said that the lodestone has soul, because it moves iron.[4]

You said we must find a new proximity, probably through pain and heartbreak. Where mint grew lustily in its pot, you receded from my listening. There are pieces of your hair still woven in carpet, but now, the house accumulates my skin and my dust.

Someone at the panel jokes,
the driving impetus for space travel is
testosterone! I escape
this body *If only I could*
Except I do every day

       dystopia (medical)
       an abnormal position
       organ or body part

I head to the desert
my arms full of
unopened mail

I can only rest when we
watch Memory Foam release
        your body pressed there
        moments before

I attend her show *Gravity Forgiveness*
I wish to see gravity forgive me
and the interstitial
crescent moons

Roads of the Dead

A card table in the library stands ready
To receive the puzzle which keeps never coming[5]

The Severan Marble Plan of Rome is a carved marble
rendering, a map of ancient Rome based on property records.
Its size complicates its ongoing digital reconstruction.

The marble map is a blueprint of every architectural
feature of the ancient city, from buildings to monuments
to staircases. The map's carved blocks once covered a wall
inside the Templum Pacis, but all surviving pieces have been
shipped to the floor of a Stanford University warehouse to be
scanned and catalogued. The 1,186 surviving marble fragments
make up only ten percent of the original marble plan. Using
3D modeling, the Computer Science department is digitally
reconstructing the whole.

The Severan Marble Plan project is a study in method.
Virtual teams of engineers, archaeologists, and researchers
from the Sovraintendenza of the City of Rome solve the
puzzle by using shape-matching algorithms to digitally
construct the jigsaw based on matching forms. That the
process is "painstaking and slow" is no deterrent.

The original plan is detailed, accurate, and consistent in scale
because it was copied from precise contemporary surveys of
the city of Rome, produced from cadastral records. Carving
mistakes and small irregularities remain in the original map.
Its reproduction is made all the more difficult because of this
lingering trace of the hand.

In the 1760s, a European mapmaker cut a wooden map of the British Empire into pieces as an educational tool for children. In the 1900s, puzzle-making attained status as an aristocratic pastime.

I'm going to Spaceport America.

To access the spaceport, I'll have to cross the Jornada del Muerto, a desert basin cut by a 100-mile road. I calculate and the Jornada del Muerto is longer than the distance between the edge of space and my body on land. Trace one expanse, maybe you'd carve across another.

The Jornada has been mapped many times, including by Google. The online map's layers include Satellite, Transit, Traffic, Biking, Terrain, Street View, Wildfires, and Air Quality. As you *approach* the area on screen, its layers reveal details.

Some few users have accessed the volcano and comment, *Scenic*, with a geotag. A user with a sad emoji suggests that the road's proximity to the Trinity Site, where the first atomic bomb was detonated, gives the Jornada its name, Road of the Dead. Another suggests the name long pre-dates this explosion.

According to the Bureau for Land Management, the Jornada Wilderness Area is *almost entirely composed of lava flows that are characterized by lava tubes, sink holes, and pressure windblown sand and clay materials, which support a variety of grass species and soaptree yucca. This area is also home to many species of dark reptiles and a large population of bats that live in a lava tube extending from a crater.*

I recall the story of Raffia, a camel who carried a camera across the Liwa Oasis in Abu Dhabi to capture terrain on video for Google Maps. When you look up videos of Raffia's footage, all you see are trains of more camels. I imagine the Jornada's *dark reptiles*. What could these be? Are they on Street View?

I want to tell you:

The name Jornada del Muerto was given by Spanish conquistadors crossing south to north from what they called New Spain to the northern viceroyalty in Santa Fe. In a great reversal, the conquerors crossed north to south in retreat during the 1680 Pueblo Revolt, one of this continent's first of many highly coordinated social revolutions.

Now the road is only crossed by a few people, including tourists.

You would quote:

No one wants to be a bad or compromised kind of force in the world, but the latter is just inevitable...The question is how to develop ways to accentuate those contradictions, to interrupt their banality and to move them somewhere.[6]

This person's coping is difficult to distinguish from an exterminating impulse. This person's ledger doesn't add up. If the constraint is a kind of boundary, then why is it so maximally invasive?

We become identified with a wound, you said, and I am like sure, let me. I persist in autobiography.

Dear _____,

Can I tell you about driving to Spaceport America? I want to take you to the site of my nightmare. To fill the seepage holes in me with the excesses in you. I want my nightmare to be your nightmare so we can finally see.

Parts for the Whole

Declarative sentences say they're straight but make out in locker rooms.

If synecdoche takes the parts for the whole, sails for a ship or threads for clothes, metonymy uses a thing to refer to another thing, a crown for a king, a suit for a man. I'm tired. The autonomous system disregulates whether or not I speak. The language for what I need folds in me like a dead thing.

I sit down to write about synecdoche but I instead receive a text containing a photograph of a bare chest. I think about my chest. What's the word when parts don't represent whole? Say, organ doesn't equal gender. A transcorporal poetics or rhetoric of elimination, a hook in a pop song. Bop bop bop.

I reply, *nice.*

I think about sending out a selfie of my chest with two holes in the middle: cut for the whole, slit for a top. There's a thing about writing to heal the body in slices, word a promissory note feeding the wildfire of feeling in the morning then stilled on a cursor, *slice.* Everyone wants something I promised.

More pics? :)

You talk about a *coming out* story. Well, mine drips slowly from my ears. It's the feeling of liquid in the wrong hole. The way I fantasize about a space hub in a desire to permeate wetly. But I forget, we're not talking, we're smearing our innards in the sheets.

Sometimes I think these things matter: whom I've loved, who I talk to, where I see myself in five years. Then I wake up and understand that culture is adjunct to the world, that it lives and dies in the present, that the archive is a *mode of governance against memory*,[7] a fantasy construction of an unknowable past. Things to remain are volcanoes, hydrogen, maybe a little river, little salt.

I read a *feelings wheel* and try to name mine: sweaty. But all I see is *mad, sad, glad,* and *bad.*

I just feel sweaty.

I rub my chest with oils and soaps and perfumes. I get touched up. Negativity is not exactly a downer, just the inverse of something. Maybe a suit. Maybe a crown for a king.

The erotics of a hand rolling
up and down jeans rhythmically
caught in a breath, I feel terse today
my paycheck feels like single ply
I email a person late
keep idioms for memos, keep a drawer
keep lists of luxuries, little pleasures
walnuts in sauce, the loud fan
of work at night. *Not today* she said
hung over from sound
beating on the brow

We Want It All so relatable, that
yes, I wanted, filling the living
room or shopping at Smith's
the way void isn't absent of yearning
the way frozen food holds potential
the way paranoid thoughts might still
substantiate, they said *Come align yourself
with splinters, come be inlaid*. My
irritant, my pain in the ass life, my bad
brief stint of lingering outside your driveway,
wanting you in a wig, wanting you
on stilts, in someone else's automatic
drive truck or on your porch in a different
season, a little colder, a little wetter, a little
unlike whatever's been good for me

I look up *Wanting for*. Mid-1600s, in
most early languages, including Norse. I'm
not without withouts, but not without
bearings, not entirely sure why
in the context of water dripped all over

my floor in the mornings drinking coffee
dripping, I'm pressing a space bar dripping
this winter long and full of capital S Secrets
little bows over silences, hot poppers in a
driveway all to myself, things that
if spoken would mire us all in action

I'm trying
to write about this thing
I can't access the feeling
might need to be pushed
bound, hit, moved, left, lost. *I want
more grace*, you said, coming off
another partial diagnosis. *I want more
Art, but I want it
at no expense*

I walk in parallel to the people on the street
they see things in this city I don't
hope in what they call tech
they have the desire to wear white gloves
produce some other place in their calculus
they seek some unsettlement for themselves
which appears the opposite of settlement But you reap
what you sow I admire
bridled with other wishes
I'm in line at the State Fair
I stay here loudly
waiting for my dessert

Fire in the Pit. Ready, Set, Go

Earth's atmosphere as it appears from space contains bands of color at the horizon. The mesosphere is pink and extends to just below the Kármán line at one hundred kilometers. The pink line of airglow of the lower thermosphere is dark, and projects green and red aurorae over several hundred kilometers. The troposphere is orange with silhouettes of clouds, and the stratosphere is white and blue.

The air is smoky from a seasonal wildfire outside Jemez.

I'm going to Spaceport America.

I pack my little blue Fiesta. I check the list of what I'll need. My mom, Doctor Mom, gets free *incentives* from drug company sponsors and medical facilities, so I scratch *gas, credit card, can-opener* off a Christus St. Vincent's Hospice notepad, Venloflaxine pen. *Oh, and my inhaler.*

Even if you were here, you would not be in charge of this doing. I am trying not to think of my systems in absence of you, or others, as my very own hospice. I am trying to eat meals in my day and fill a water bottle according to some internal clock of care, what magazines call self-regulation, a habit I've picked up to keep distant from those who insist on doing these things together. With you, I can speak freely in my little microphone. I can leave my house, tell no one, make my way through this compulsion of story for some future telling. I make sandwiches. I like hot fries on the road. Whatever. I sit in the front seat with my steroid medication, inhale, hold my breath, think about fire season.

Back in 2000, an uncontrolled fire, the Cerro Grande, started near the Los Alamos National Lab's Plutonium Facility, approaching its "Area G" radioactive dump. Fire and winds stirred up the release of airborne contaminants, propelling waste sediment into watershed drainage that feeds the Rio Grande. In national news outlets, anxieties erupted about nuclear meltdown, *what happens if the fire cannot be contained, what if the lab must be abandoned?*

Particles from leaking laboratory transformers contaminated the watershed, raising the Rio Grande river's levels of polychlorinated biphenyls (PCBs), Cesium 137, plutonium and cyanide. From my home in Santa Fe, the smoke was thick and relentless, as were stories of high school friends' houses in Los Alamos burnt to the ground. We got to know FEMA, who left quickly. The enduring damage was slower, more invisible.

GPS. 54 hours to walk to Truth or Consequences, near Spaceport A. Today, 2 hours, 11 minutes by car. Easy. I'll need a room for one night, maybe a few, I'm not sure what I'll find or how long I'll need to see this through. Google recommends Rocket Inn. I count what's free, even what may be expected to be free. I learn this from my parents. Free breakfast. Free Wi-fi. Free coffee. Free towels. 4.6 stars. Barb H. wins me over. *Rocket Inn is quiet, the decor is attractive and inviting, and the owners provide friendly, exceptional service.* I'm eating snacks that cover my fingers in red dust.

You call reviews "micro memoir." Yelp is the top publisher of this genre. *Why do I say the service is exceptional? Well, after our recent stay I discovered I had forgotten my purse (yes, credit cards, ID, cash, everything) in the room. But the time I realized it we were 2 hours away. I called Cydney (one of the owners) who immediately went*

to our room and located my purse. After discussing several options, we
agreed she'd send it to me via priority mail and would email me the
tracking number. As I told Cydney when I received my purse in the
mail, "You saved me not only time and money but also mental anguish
at the thought of my personal and financial documents in the wrong
hands. It is very clear that you operate with integrity and honesty."

Emergency landing, you would say. I book, in a few taps,
Rocket Inn, since Google remembers my card. After all this,
I think, I'll leave a review better than Barb's, find use for
exceptional service. I'm sure of it. I'll call it, *My Time During*
Your Time on Mars. Or maybe some other math equation.

In the aftermath of the Cerro Grande fire, nuclear waste
storage became, briefly, a national conversation. The
Concerned Citizens for Nuclear Safety and Nuclear Policy
Project released an executive summary of concerns in fire's
aftermath, notes I read on their online bulletin. They flag
disposal pits, burial grounds, underground tanks, *hundreds*
of shafts filled with radioactive and hazardous wastes that have
accumulated for more than a half century near Los Alamos
National Labs. There are still over 2,120 potential radiation
release sites near the laboratory.

I know how radioactive rock and fluid, or uranium mill
tailings, dot the northwestern corner of New Mexico,
radiating from mining sites under smoke, or crystal clear
skies. I know this somehow in my flesh, from childhood,
my early collision in body with this story, these memories
tumbling out while I try to sleep, or bicker over who pays a
bill. I try to tell stories at things like lunch, or a lecture. On
Tinder, at a birthday, but there's a vague dis-ease in doing
so, like the function just goes to zero. I have this plastic

Venloflaxine pen. Or a memo, the grain of a voice box,
and you.

If I can make it to
The headlines

*For decades the Los Alamos National Laboratory has steeled itself
against the possibility of a nuclear missile strike. It has guarded
against terrorists, spies and computer hackers. But the threat that
turned out to be most immediate was disquietingly familiar: the
tens of thousands of acres of neighboring Ponderosa forests that crowd
the Pajarito plateau and the adjacent Jemez mountains, and which
exploded, as had long been feared, into a firestorm.*[8]

Since then, we've had numerous fires.

Earlier this year, I waited at my grandparents' house, bags
packed, scrolling Facebook comments and crowdsourcing
emergency preparedness tips, questions rolling on our watch
over the uncontrolled fire north of their land in El Rito. We
sat on the brink at *ready, set*. Edging. At this moment, my
dad crumpled completely, declaring he has no particular
objects to save, no photo albums to shove in the back of our
car. An old bible I dangle in two fingers is rejected with the
swiftest dismissal. *I thought this family tree mattered to someone?
It was supposed to be a list of our male relatives? Nevermind.* We're
outside trimming branches and beating spring's new growth
back from the house, trying to save it all in hilarious fashion.
Remove wood and wicker furniture from porch, a Facebook user
writes. *Clear your brush.*

Go. Dumb little Ford.

Driving through a smoky haze, I think about whether our emergency containment plans are built for some imagined system that does not change, a kind of fantasy land of order and stasis. What is this fictional ecosystem, this land, where emergency is the unexpected intervention, not the course of things, like a fire, a thing the land does, at random, all the time? How can you contain a landed material reality subject to—no, *comprised of* change? How can you even calculate where to store plutonium waste, above, below, shifting boundaries.

Archeologists still debate what drove the Anasazi from their stone settlements. Drought, warfare, boredom—no one really knows. The abandonment of Los Alamos was brief and the ruins will be rebuilt. But it's hard to escape the conclusion that the modern settlers were driven off the plateau by the cumulative force of their leaders' own actions and indecisions. And by the illusion that they were in control.

Karen Barad writes, *Lightning is a reaching toward, an arcing dis/juncture, a striking response to charged yearnings.*[9] Chaos, a name assigned to systems, both nonlinear and complex linear, is used to describe an irregular and unpredictable temporal evolution, the point at which stability moves to instability or order moves to disorder. Fire is a consuming expansion, a furious activation of fuel and energy.

Some things we cannot write at all, because they can't be contained or predicted, sensitive as they are to their initial conditions and what happens afterward, each contextual shift. In the end, you acted like I didn't even try, like nothing I felt one moment mattered more than what I felt the next. I, too, have unruly attachments that form the basis of longing, and I guess, too, this errant telling. Still I wanted more kindness, even in the truths.

Leaving this place they tell me

It's suburbs

It's a development

Your natural piece of my plan

I built an opera

in my mind

to play while you're talking

to keep out the letters

floating towards me

I see signs

I want to

be your swill

I hit the mark

told you I hit the mark

then I told the whole world

I realize that despite our bad blood

This is a love story

I display on my countertop

the fantasies that can be shared

@BadUtopian

I like her handle

I imagine our conversation

> @BadUtopian
>
> this year is going to be so much better than last year
>
> @Halcyondais @BadUtopian
>
> fool me once but
>
> the way you make sentences
>
> the way egg gels
>
> you cool
>
> I melt
>
> let me slide into your DMs
>
> @BadUtopian
>
> I wish to
>
> Baby, just
>
> yes

exosphere.

thermosphere.

mesosphere.

stratosphere.

troposphere.

I may have blown my cover
I may have told you I don't care
which is obviously a tell
for caring way too much

This town feels like space
because we died
left our lives behind
we didn't know where else
to lay our median

In space there's a Mac Store
up the road the mall, monochrome
tinsel. Sun fades a forgotten fuzz
I take refuge, our date at Cottonwood
once white now soot

Jiffy Lube, you confessed you walked
sunsets, moved in corridors
your long tunnel to Sushi King
old streets with your name
family feuds 300 years prior

We're pumping gas now
the ones you still
look in the eye

Uranium Yellow

I drive south on I-25, ten miles over the speed limit.

I suck sunflower seeds, salty, sing to the radio—*baby your song*—until it turns to static. I listen to the static to distract from my own thoughts, until I'd rather remember everything that has ever happened. Roughly five minutes. So now I am thinking about here. Specifically *here*. I have not lived in-state for ten years. Yet it's where my body knows home. It is, at least, where belonging was first negotiated in my nervous system.

Mei-mei Berssenbrugge writes, *When your experience ardently links to an object or person where you live—husband, tree, stone—you try to hold onto the visibility of this object and its location.*

But I wish to evacuate.

My parents moved to Shiprock, NM, when I was less than a year old. I believe they intended to stay for one to two years, but remained for seven. My mother was a doctor for uranium miners. Her patients endured cancers from lifelong exposure to radiation. I believe my parents figured this period contained, like a neat house. The work, outside. Our family inside. Or perhaps they didn't think, just did—work, run labs, make lists, write scripts. Then call governors, meet with lawyers, talk renumeration. Things, political.

School photo day, my combed blonde hair blobbing visible and unnecessary in the hall. Home, my parents young, limber and brunette, overworked, cooking mashed potatoes. Grief-stricken, my dad's brother has killed himself.

Do we or *are we allowed* to refuse coalescing language around those foundational experiences that form our sense of the world? Can we tell a story by other means?

Most uranium deposits are found near the Four Corners, where Colorado, New Mexico, Arizona, and Utah touch each other. Uranium mining for nuclear bomb production is this place's secret story, *a deadly legacy, for which the government has only begun to make amends.*

It's an eternally unfulfilled wish, that governments could make amends.

I want to ask, what do colors look like on your Mars. Is your yellow still yellow in the simulation?

Of course it is, you'd say. *It's Earth.*

Most people know uranium to be yellow. Its natural color is a dark silvery-gray. When uranium is in a compound with oxygen, it forms a yellow oxide called uranyl peroxide. The peroxide group contributes to the color by causing a shift in the electronic structure of the uranium atom, affecting the way it interacts with light. The yellow of uranyl peroxide is produced through the absorption of certain wavelengths of light by the compound, and the reflection of yellow light. The uranium atom in uranyl peroxide has an oxidation state of +6, meaning it has lost six electrons from its natural state and is now highly reactive.

If you were here, I'd tell you about Demian DinéYazhi´, whose sculpture *my ancestors will not let me forget this* is uranium yellow.[10] Installed at the 2019 Honolulu Biennial, the work is all neon signage, aluminum, and insulated wiring.

It illuminates:

EVERY
AMERICAN FLAG
IS A WARNING SIGN

On the radio, a man, I think he calls himself a neurobiologist,
says, *we are thinking a lot about mindset.* The research proves that
our relationship to stress determines our physiological response
to stress. I zone out for a moment. I will try to love stress,
I decide.

I know about a whole history of relations with my body.
But I've forgotten my body, substituted its telling for some other
stories, partial, compelling, alienated, remote. Easier. I admire
DinéYazhi´'s artwork and what it does to my body. I note its
activation energy (n., chemistry, 1889), *the minimum quantity of
energy which the reacting species must possess in order to undergo a
specified reaction.*

The first time I heard the words I didn't know what they meant.

The hundredth time I heard them, fireworks of mutiny
detonated behind my eyelids.
Uranium poisoning.

Last year, in Albuquerque, I'd gone to a dance party to *de-stress.*
A man unknown to anyone got in a fight and had to be escorted
out. When he came back with a gun, a butch cook shuffled us
through the back door. We were crouching in a scene I thought
could appear as cell phone footage. *We're going down, should I text
someone?* I wanted to text the cook. Later we learned he did not
have a gun, but a machete. Later we learned the police had him
on the ground outside for hours.

The southwestern US is constructed in layers. These layers are histories of here, of elsewhere, of colonial inheritance—names, dates, stories, treaties, contracts, coordinates, signs. This desert basin, here, or volcano crater, there, exist outside language—yet they've become *places*, narrated by discourses of nation, produced through imaginaries of space.

I notice you look to scale
I notice before we get started

Vocation reduced to labor
stings so often settled time drags
In the night outside script sometimes
the road has no cover

If you'd been in the car at this point, we'd have stopped at the Very Large Array. *Contact* holds a sway I admit I associate with someone else, but I'd stop anyway, with company. *You've seen it: a giant field of 27 white radio telescopes, mounted on railroad tracks, all turned toward the sky.*[11]

Instead I pull off to Walgreens, listening, in the parking lot, to their classical music aggress. I sit in the car and watch people go in and out. When I enter, everything is behind plastic locks.

I have only read the golden lettering of DinéYazhi´'s sculpture in the blue light of my laptop, but the block of text is alive, not only in the way all matter is alive (*What makes us think that matter is lifeless to begin with*[12]), but also in the way an electric current passes through and animates neon gas, exciting it into emitting a bright orange light.

Electroluminescence. In Walgreens, Takis Blue Heat look poisonous, but I know blue is the secret best flavor.

Fluorescence. Natural uranium does not glow in the dark, but under certain conditions, it can emit light. When uranium is exposed to UV light, it absorbs the energy and re-emits it as visible light, giving off a bluish glow.

Radioactivity. Uranium glow isn't radioactivity. The radioactivity is actually the emission of particles from the nucleus of the unstable atom, which can cause damage to cells, DNA, and tissues. This leads to radiation sickness and cancer.

Back on the road, I turn up radio static, ignoring thoughts of damage. I imagine the sculpture's electric hum and remind myself that the excitation of atoms is a promiscuous material process, a response to energy coming in and stimulating what's already there. I whir at the thought, remembering why I've returned to New Mexico after ten years away.

I still feel the burn of where you touched my gut. I try not to go back to that time in my mind, but memory plays like a movie reel and distorts my sense of the present.

There's something infantilizing about the life I lead now, bare feet on carpet, beer half drunk in the fridge. I'm here. I live in this town. I've left the tag on my shirt. *Oh it must be beautiful* they say, referring to *36 Hours in* ——, or a postcard. Or perhaps they visited in 2004.

I pass a billboard for a personal injury lawyer. I swipe right on a Tinder bio that says, *I ain't good.*

Where you go today
I'll see you in your environs
where *Did that shop close*
I'm craning my damn
I avoid the highway

I read you the way I walk these lanes
here but not here, here *But 100 years ago*
and I'm reading
100 years ago, here
But there's so much
history, and this lot

There are ways to be in love
with how blistering hot
how workaday where
I'm reading my stories
and looking for shade

How maddening, the yous standing in for you
At this point I could laser them off
like moles
You're my benign skin flap
the bit of me I knew was
almost alien
I think I did you
wrong once

What pains
in my approach
is something puts me on trial
Here
I do my best over text
I've been here before

I'm in a former seabed, awaiting
the moon's full funeral rites
I pay bills well into the future
with credit from times of plenty

Someday for Free.99
I'll be an ash sampler
out Earth orbit sprayed
where the moon is ill and I
have no sense of periodicity

I've mourned your passage
and I'll do it again in fiction
where sleeping dogs
howl at the moon

Discretion Time

I try composing in response to some imagined question.

Are cognitive processes different from feelings?

But all I can think of is your face approaching mine.

This is distracting as I try to think about theory. I don't think my body is cut out for theory. It is cut out for approaching what is incoming. Your face in my mind.

I have a vision of how bodies overlap at three feet apart. I'm sitting here and you're there and we're already beaming, which is my theory of noticing (you). I am indiscrete.

Indiscretion is a spatial word. *Discretio* means separation and *discern*, to separate out.

We discern based on wealth, sex, gender, race, mood, inbox, file. That is measure by distinction, a kind of systemic fiction. We put things in their places, windows, categories. But I am not. Every day I am clocked as imprecise and unwillingly contained. "I" try to discuss that my containment may be a limiting fiction, but they call me, probably, disgusting.

Next to you, I am indiscrete in theory. I don't know about cognitive processes. What's more I have a feeling. There's something so concrete as a finger, yours, hanging on your lips. Me, noticing. Us, already related. The car, not the boundary it seems.

It's so precise, my knowing.

I walk around the edges of a room
I put this strap on

I walk around the edges of a room
I feel a crease in my mattress

I walk up the walls of the room
What do you know about

That isn't knowledge per se
I want to know

Baby your song
It makes me wanna

Roll my windows
Down and cruise[13]

The One Who Has Met or Encountered the Other

Spaceport America, formerly known as the Southwest Regional Spaceport, is owned by the state of New Mexico through a state agency, the New Mexico Spaceport Authority. It was designed and constructed for commercial, *non-state* users. Shifting government-run space missions to commercial ventures is tricky business. Rocketry was always paid for and developed by the US military. Rocketry is ballistics.

In ballistics or aerodynamics, an *ogive* (/ˈoʊdʒaɪv/ OH-jive) is a pointed, curved surface, the roundly tapered end of a two- or three-dimensional object, used mainly to form the approximately streamlined nose of a bullet, rocket, or other projectile, reducing the drag of air.

The earliest use of *ogive* is from a thirteenth-century sketchbook by Villard de Honnecourt, from Picardy, northern France, a man known only for this surviving book of technical procedures and objects. The Oxford English Dictionary considers the ogive's origin obscure, perhaps evolving from the Late Latin *obviata*, the feminine perfect passive participle of *obviare*, meaning—

The one who has met or encountered the other.

Theodore von Kármán, one of the most influential figures in aerodynamics, was presented with the first-ever Medal of Science by US President John F. Kennedy. There's a photograph of von Kármán meeting the president in 1963 at an inaugural award ceremony. Next to von Kármán perched at a microphone, JFK towers, lean and handsome in a pencil-thin tie and black suit. Von Kármán, small, hands in his pockets, faces an audience in a calf-length black trench coat. Three months after this photograph is taken, Theodore von Kármán dies at age 81. Six months after this photograph is taken, President John F. Kennedy is assassinated.

Midway to my driving destination, I notice that billboards stripped of last year's advertisements glance empty and comical off my windshield. Slow and dusty, windy in scattered bursts, this place feels like capitalism glitched. I hardly see a soul.

In the von Kármán papers at Caltech, the collected photographs reveal a life dedicated to shiny machines. There's the photograph of the Modane Wind Tunnel in St. Louis, France. Blaue Maus and Schwarzer Duwel, a small aeroplane propped up in a studio on stools, disassembled, or in the process of assembly. There's the large glider on the ground, and Weltrekord Klemperer, the small plane aloft. There's the Ercoupe with jet-assisted take off, and the Boeing Model 247 monoplanes under construction. And there's an old print of T. S. C. Lowe's balloon, used by the Union Amy during the American Civil War.

I am driving towards someplace someone once called *empty*. My drive south flies by, belying the drag of time in the landscape around me.

Southern New Mexico doesn't at first seem like a land of big economic ventures. People keep to themselves. They signal across streets, kind of nod and go about their business. I mean, so much more than that, but codes are not about, say, France, international travel or self-driving cars, or maybe especially not silicone injections, or new words for old things, technologies like language busting out of its containers. I base these ruminations off my thoughts when I lived here, a kind of meandering life-wish to leave and never leave at the same time, that gets me back in when I get out. I resist everything changing.

Social narratives of certain spaces as *empty* are prevalent in the national imaginaries of colonial nations. These *wastelanded* areas are, paradoxically, *vital*, for the colonial project. [14]

In her study of nuclear imperialism in French-Algerian relations, Roxanne Panchasi writes that Algeria, under French colonial rule, was called *vital territory*—

...where nuclear tests might be conducted far from the metropolitan French population. [15]

According to Panchasi, this was *one of many arguments against any [French] withdrawal from Algeria.* The remoteness of the edge to the center, and the ideologies of emptiness imposed on its locale, were some of Algeria's values to the nation of France.

I'm driving towards someplace someone once called *empty*.

A closeup photograph titled *Theodore von Kármán at blackboard, with cigar* captures von Kármán writing an equation at a chalkboard ($L = grv...$), a midsized cigar perched and ashing between two fingers. A portrait titled *Theodore von Kármán with his bust* depicts von Kármán standing next to a stone carving of his own head (no neck). Von Kármán wears a full tuxedo complete with a bow tie, looking quite like his bust.

I certainly didn't dream of kaleidoscopic unrest. Didn't dream of this body, unruly and fidgety. Didn't set out for so much more than lunch. But there's an overmuch news cycle, with a crushing racket of blows. Who can stand a more acute awareness in this oversaturated space?

Anyone without enough language (still), or anyone flying down the highway. Anyone looking for words, such as new words for an old story:

I am driving towards someplace someone once called *empty*. Empty enough to detonate an atomic bomb.

Complex ogives can be derived from minimum turbulence calculations rather than from geometric forms. The von Kármán ogive used for supersonic missiles, aircraft and bullets calculates the ideal shape of a tapered cone using calculations pertaining to the cone's surrounding air—what we *might* think of as the negative space or surround, only this is air. Agitated, it pulls—buffets, *drags*. This calculation, all to produce *the one who has met or encountered the other*.

Air is hardly empty.

Throughout his life, von Kármán worked closely with the US military. He designed aircraft and spacecraft, including the first all-metal aircraft and the World War II P-47 Thunderbolt fighter plane. In 1944, upon receiving reports about German scientists working on military rockets, the US Army contracted with von Kármán at Caltech to manufacture weapons. Von Kármán founded the Jet Propulsion Laboratory, which later developed spacecraft for NASA. He chaired the Air Force Scientific Advisory Board, which in 1945 charted a theory of post-war military systems, anticipating supersonic flight, intercontinental ballistic missiles, surface-to-air missiles, and nuclear warheads.

And he envisaged the Kármán line, this imaginary threshold, this edge of space.

I know enough to know that AirBnbs dot this landscape. Their tucked-away glitz sits invisible next to yards cluttered with rusted car parts. Borders distribute themselves across social contexts here. In the same space, invisible lines police the values and energies of the next door down. *Layers*. Electric fence. Wireless perimeter. Borders made up of languages, customs, speech. Doorbell camera. We want to be isolated, we contain ourselves, fear contact.

Then find ourselves lonely.

There's an allure to analogy. (An edge can be so many things.) But in thinking about it, I wrestle against an enticing wrongness.

Analogy means we're substituting one thing for another, talking *as if*, talking *like*. Is space an analogy for our beliefs, or is it an active presence, a dynamic field? Even metonymy is an Achilles' heel and my turn away produces a baroque quality of thinking. I flirt hard with discomfort. There's an erotics to this struggle.

I want to dwell in space, that is, live.

Untethered, unbothered, yeah.

But can we even calculate the shape of the ogive—*that*

penetrating vessel—in a void of language, empty of story, history? What is intimacy without material space?

We need a language of turbulence to calculate our shape.

Backscatter

The Belt of Venus, also called Venus's Girdle, is an atmospheric phenomenon visible shortly before sunrise or after sunset, during civil twilight. It's the pinkish glow that surrounds an observer, extending roughly 10–20° above the horizon.

My windshield looks like paintings or a dry erase board.
I take a photo, post it on my story, 45 minutes from the end of my drive. I'll park, stay the night, get on my tour. I'll probably text, or maybe I won't.

I'll definitely compose a text. *Will I send?*

Here's a photo of an alien sticker on the back of some guy's trailer.

You *like* this.

I could write volumes.

In March of this year, I pulled up YouTube Live to watch Falcon 9's launch of the Iridium-5 mission, SpaceX's tenth flight of a previously flown (recycled) rocket. Ten satellites were to be delivered and deployed to low-Earth orbit for Iridium, a satellite constellation.

Iridium, *the only satellite network that allows you to send out an immediate SOS from anywhere on Earth.*

I'd heard about Iridium flares, where the sun reflects off one of the satellites' flat, door-sized antenna arrays in the exosphere. These are sometimes visible in one bright flash from the ground. A man who worked at NASA once said, *I saw one by accident. It looks like a police spotlight, WAY up there.*

I wish in this moment to see one for myself—a seconds-long burst of police that outshines the planet Venus.

Back in the spring, I watched comments roll as the Iridium-5 launch mission counted down on YouTube. Anticipation seemed to turn to boredom as the time rolled on. But then, the rocket's wings came out. The mood shifted. Comments took a dark, frantic turn.

Don't blow it up. Pray for them. Avatars hedged and fussed.

As I drive, I review in my head the various offerings available to the dead at Spaceport America. I'd read on Spaceport website that these unique funeral services are available to honor loved ones with a *far out sendoff.*

> You can purchase the Earth Rise Service, which allows you to send a symbolic portion of your dead loved one into space. They experience zero gravity and are returned to Earth.

> You can purchase the Earth Orbit Service, which places your loved one in orbit on the Celestis rocket where their DNA floats until it reenters the atmosphere burning up on entry and costs a little more.

> You can order the Luna Service, which places your loved one's *cremains* on the moon, *the surface of our nearest neighbor,* and costs a little more.

$12,500 is somehow less than I'd expected. Two cars in the rearview, I imagine funeral services that could be ignited by Celestis Memorial Spaceflights.

In a serene and dry, modern setting in the New Mexico desert, family and friends gather at the carefully chosen launch site. Anticipation is palpable, mingling with a sense of sorrow and wonder. The surroundings are serene under a breathtaking, unending sky. Attendees find solace in the beauty and tranquility of the notion of the cosmos. Guests prepare to bid farewell to their loved one.

The service begins with a procession, with attendees walking together in unity towards the launchpad. As the group approaches, gentle music fills the air. Adorned with the Celestis insignia and personalized tributes, the waiting rocket stands ready, a symbol of remembrance and also hope, for a future beyond this world. A speaker steps forward, offering comforting words and reflections for a life departed. The speaker shares memories, and anecdotes, all positive. These stories evoke tears and smiles. A vivid picture is painted of the beloved. The speaker's voice resonates, carrying their words as waves across the launch site and through the atmosphere.

My great-aunt was a rancher in La Madera, New Mexico. I remember my great-aunt's memorial. Her childhood asthma brought her parents west for the air, then brought my grandparents, my parents. These are colonial stories, familial, personal, historical, social, structural. Neighboring ranchers called my great-aunt *Doña Jona*. And also, *Crazy, loca*. She was never far from her shotgun.

Joan Atterbury ran 300 head of cattle across acres hundreds of acres of juniper forest for most of her life. She married her ranch hand. As a younger woman, she was raped on the side of the road by a group of men passing in a car. As children, we sprinkled her ashes on the dirt ground of her ranch in the shape of a long cross.

I don't know what to do with these stories. So many communities' relatives have walked these lands. I drive, asking what have rites ushered them through this here, if not also beyond?

To think—already, some beings are being sent skywards, not returning to the Earth.

> *Perhaps for an extra fee, a visiting astronaut follows.*

> *Perhaps, this astronaut offers a speech describing the science and miracle of liftoff.*

At the moment of ignition, the Iridium-5's Falcon 9 rocket engines, pixelated, roared to life on my screen. In the browser's lingering feed, flames erupted from rocket base. Billowing clouds of smoke and steam engulfed the launchpad.

Watching the livestream, I'd wished hard at that moment for some newsreel—some teleprompter, or polyphonic chorus—put together a meaningful narrative. Not the emoji, or the rush of hearts, but some words, maybe a story of the complexities of *occupancy* and *occupation*; a text box, a tickertape; a convulsion of new narratives.

The Belt of Venus is like the alpenglow visible near the horizon during twilight, a backscatter of reddened sunlight so familiar, it hardly bears remark. I've seen it included, by happenstance, on nearly every painting of a mountainscape, sunlight scattered by fine particulates causing the rouged arch of the Belt to shine high in the atmosphere after sunset or before sunrise.

Miles on, the painting in my windshield becomes less lineated. Figures or shadows dance convex on its plane.

Es freue sich
Wer da atmet im rosigten Licht[16]

Let him rejoice
Who breathes up here in the roseate light

exosphere.

thermosphere.

mesosphere.

stratosphere.

troposphere.

The Kármán Line

In principle, calculating the latitude of the Kármán line for any planet is simple. For some planet of mass M the orbital speed $v_o(r)$ at a distance r from the center of the planet is just:

$$v_o(r)=\sqrt{GMr}$$

Where G is the gravitational constant. From here it gets messier. If you're flying a plane with some mass m, then the gravitational force pulling you down is (this is just Newton's equation):

$$Fg=GMmr^2$$

Using the expression for the lift, the lift opposing the gravitation force is:

$$F_{lift}=1/2\rho v^2 AC_L$$

To work out what speed you need to fly, set $Fg=F_{lift}$ and you get (after a bit of rearrangement):

$$vfly(r)=\sqrt{2GMmpACLr2}$$

The Kármán line is the height at which $vo(r)=v_{fly}(r)$. Setting these equal and removing the common factors of G, M, and r gives:

$$2m\rho(r)AC_L r=1$$

This is a simple equation and solving for r gives you the height of the Kármán line. The problem is that the atmosphere density $\rho(r)$ is a function of height, and it varies in a non-trivial way because it depends on the temperature and the temperature varies in a non-trivial way with height. To work out the Kármán line on an extraterrestrial planet I suspect you'd need to know the temperature.

Still in place despite great
love poems there founded

Here under the edge
no fault but your affect

I say, *What do you mean*
that this problem is

Mine, that your edge pokes
my under-armpit skin

That no sleep is possible
when it's raining all over

My roof ? Unprepared
I'm going to need to wait

I get going, sign all the papers
scheme this period's purpose

My cognitive dissonance
the thing required

I fold neatly
into a day

Cowboy poem, gender being
a motor left running

A car out back
waiting for groceries

My exhaust
stinking up

A perfectly
good driveway

Sound Bodily Condition

Your industry-standard vinyl liner may line the deep concrete shell of your swimming pool in the desert. Your Secret Swimming Pool in the Mojave may populate my image search 3,000 km from the site of my casual roving.

In order to escape the feeling of the day, I look up at the ceiling. I know when I arrive I'll address injury. At the same time I'll address takeoff. At the same time I'll discuss why I've been drinking from your faucet and eating your leftovers.

I don't want to get outside of the speculative and abstract. Writing so easily becomes about naming. More than any other art form, writing is tied to classification because its medium is language. When I talk about violence, this relationship or that, tie it to my life, a person, an experience, I've diagnosed a problem I had no wish to diagnose.

Without social cues, requirements—duties which muscle us into our regulated shapes—I find myself somewhere out there, where casual intimacy shimmers with possibility and clutter. In space more than anywhere, I want to tap your forehead or shoulder or rib until you breathe deep from it. I want to learn how to get at the thing I don't yet know, the blank space in memory, the experiences I should have language for and don't. The reasons I can no longer address you or you, the instinct I've had to flee the scene or risk losing my cohesiveness. The lack of space, the too much space.

The way sex, another way of saying culture, one connected to whiteness and coloniality, with its prescriptions of gender and race, absolutely inscribed in space, the way it pushes you down into its medium like a screw in hard wood. Gripping tightly but not remotely part of, not viscous, not fluid on fluid. People talk about betweenness as a new system of classification. You can't believe in it until you're face down on someone's bed wondering why your experience has been excruciating. Until you're wondering what you don't know you don't know, how everything you've been taught led you to this place.

An interest in space in fact might be dissociative, a tool deployed in the throes of contact, which is no contact, too much of the wrong contact. But I don't know how to meet outside of outside. I leave some people there in the remove and I call out to them sometimes, crying, it's lonely here without their corroborations. Skipping out to the metaphor of a house, a room, furnishings, things in boxes, stuff piled everywhere, stepping out to try to describe a thing without naming it, give the mood of it. What's a painterly approach worth?

If only you were to see, there's no diagnosis for consciousness and even worse, none for the unconscious however we belabor its dredging. Beyond that and better, no way of knowing my body in its viscosity and its thousand breakages without taking off your glasses and feeling it all out with your hands.

If you think this ache in the body has nothing to do with environment, you're wrong. If you think this ache in the body has nothing to do with the malaise you feel when you wake up, scroll, make toast, scroll, turn on the heat, scroll. When you paste your pasty white over scroll scroll scroll, take a body, usury. Take something, from someone, *a direction*.

To return to environment, I delineate the body context.

Having felt the rain a cold black drench and recalling the taste of you on my fingers, I pull my car over on the highway. What I ask, is for you to stop naming and making precise the site of mourning. I cut to Secret Swimming Pool in the Mojave.jpg to stop myself thinking of this, of you. I merge with traffic.

You walk the stretch of this sidewalk. Precisely, you walk up and down. You drop into the empty pool bed, run its length. You chew gum and walk, you do a two hands thing and walk. Ultimately, you are coordinated. You super move. You are the motile equivalent of a correct wind. But you have *no* idea where you are going.

The greater ill than claim is detachment.

Which stakes out the territory of monied placelessness. That is a property of the imaginary with walled compartment containing of past wrongdoing, a box, the bad, moist historical seizure sealed in the bad, the box. Instead, we make our history in the present in the ongoing real context of this tile, a simple infrastructure in this unpolished downtown. The where of this somewhere is a good nightmare that holds, not in false fixity but in a web of meaning, touching at me imprecisely.

You *wish* you could float in placelessness like a mechanic empire of eros, but do you? That unwellness. Meanwhile, talk on the street of asteroid mining.

I see invisible threads tying me to night, space, the arc of morning across the tile, this slant, regardless of violence, regardless of corrosive salivation of past forefathers, a misnomer. They were never my father. However I might disavow or claim them, they are something utterly different than that.

You are signaling a belonging, here, in this place, outside contractual ownership. *Oh I have papers*, you might say, *but I don't believe in it.*

Well, then don't.

Can I tell you about driving to Spaceport America?

Your industry-standard vinyl liner may line the deep concrete shell of your swimming pool in the desert. Your Secret Swimming Pool in the Mojave may populate the image search 3,000 km from the site of your casual roving.

As the plane banked over urban sprawl, my eyes were caught by the turquoise glitter of all the backyard swimming pools.[17]

You're home
but never in my bed.
A problem arises,
your prior directionality

I hand over money
admit the truth, I sit in the crux
of desire and orientation
with bigger fish to fry

I try to pet you
a form of tolerance.
Domed by you
I face what's familial

Aspects of me
you, here
I hold suspended
in art, judgment
gets to take a break

Low and behold
anything withstands
being cross cut
by a line

I go to the store
find my purchase *Here*
I say, handing you far too much.
Next time I see you
Wear it

I don't encounter you
without some retroactive harm, recalling
this desire or that pasted
on a blue wall, a post
an old European road tagged
in merry mention. I admit

I didn't go back
boxed you up, a long brown trail of
dry rosemary

Rocket Inn

Comets portend fire, wind, war, famine, and death.

Most early treatises on space focus on the meaning of celestial events as pertaining to *life on Earth*. The *Kometenbuch* (*Comet Book*), anonymous, France, 1587, focuses on the meaning of comets for terrestrial beings, a lane of medieval philosophy focused on *disaster* (n. Latin, meaning *bad star*).

Comet oh damn it, you sang.

I roll into the Rocket Inn in Truth or Consequences, New Mexico, the city closest to Spaceport America's rocket launch facility. Out front a neon VACANCY sign glows under a rectangular lightbox proclaiming the motel's name, ROCKET INN, a toy rocket shooting between the two words.

Purple and yellow color scheme like a Planet Fitness. I drive up.

Motel-style, my door opens to the outside of a gravel driveway. My room is decorated cutely. On the bed there's a pillow, teal and orange, with STARS written across the top in block lettering. There's a throw quilt, a spikey atomic design, in teal and orange atop white bedding. The tissue paper box matches the bedding. I take my inhaler. Pet dander.

Motels always have pet fur, the unspoken rule of doors that open to the outside.

I want to write you, *I'm in Rocket Inn, T or C, at long last. Spaceport A tomorrow*. Because you would understand how it feels. Like a local tourist, a New Yorker in Times Square.

I've been planning this journey ever since I read about the commercial space industry coming to New Mexico.

I'd send you a postcard. *Thinking of you!*
Cute, like a 1950s ad. Like watching the moon landing on *Mad Men*.

The Spaceport venture in New Mexico feels like it was essentially a failure. That Virgin Galactic, the company it was constructed for, recently transferred its business to the Mojave Air and Space Port launchpad in California, that the New Mexico spaceport primarily hosts school science contests, the government millions in the hole, is no surprise and no real deterrent. This only adds to its appeal, makes it more local. Our social services may lack—but we have an economic plan that exists as potential, as a dream, a kind of weird, bad dream.

Like most capitalist dreams, it's given us another place to sell postcards.

The early *Kometenbuch*'s chapters reference an older book, written around 1238 in Spain, on the Earthly meaning of comets. One of the few remaining illustrated copies of the *Kometenbuch* survived a WWII air raid, in which Allied planes bombed Kassel, Germany. The bombing destroyed 350,000, or around 90 percent, of the State Library's books.

Aurora comet: *A city rages with fire.*

I adjust my postcard fantasy.
Wish you were here! Lipstick kiss. Minus the lipstick.
But then where's the kiss?

Thinking of you, writing
against time and erosion. Something
so simple: Your last sentence

I read about the medieval *Kometenbuch*, folding myself into a
pretzel on the bed. Truth or Consequences has a dark comet
history, tales I don't particularly wish to recall, but which
cling to several small towns south of Albuquerque.

I lurk in the room's cool dimness.

Truth or Consequences, formerly Hot Springs, New Mexico,
got its name from the radio. Ralph Edwards, the host of a
popular NBC Radio quiz show, made an announcement.
The program would be broadcast from the first town to
rename itself after the show on its tenth anniversary. The
town voted, and Hot Springs officially changed its name on
March 31, 1950.

The following evening, the show aired—from the newly
named Truth or Consequences.

Renowned for its thermal springs, Truth or Consequences
became known nationally when its first public hot bath was
established in the late 1800s. The springs were called Geronimo.

Geronimo Springs.

In the *Kometenbuch*, fantastical illustrations of comets mirror
textual descriptions. Full-page scenes blaze with fiery rocks,
some with faces, hurling into dazzling heavens above dark
landscapes. The descending rocks read like omens of disaster
announcing themselves in the night.

*"Veru" as a lance, "Domina capillorum" as burning wheel, "Rosa"
with beaming face, and "Scutella" as some kind of heavenly Asclepius'
staff... In the print for "Aurora," which was thought to be an omen of
impending conflagrations, a city rages with fire.*

Geronimo, also, Goyaałé, an infamous leader of the
Bedonkohe band of the Ndendahe Apache people, was held
and tortured by the US government as a prisoner of war.

Before that, Geronimo led Apache resistance against US
military campaigns on Apache lands. The raids took place
during an extended conflict between the US and the Apache,
who resisted forced containment by the US government on
segregated reservation lands. Geronimo headed up several
battles against Mexican and US forces, with aims to return
his people to nomadic life on their own lands. He was
eventually captured.

Geronimo Springs is now the name of a 3,578-mile San
Antonio real estate development.

> I thought art
> was something
> who is angry
>
> Or pointing
> to the scar language
> bears its histories

I don't know what I need.

I adjust my position on the bed. Rocket Inn hums outside, a
generator—or an unidentified being.

I am tired. Of scooping you out of oblivion—that obscurity of your, or my, making.

You are writing about Mars, a bizarre twist that's made everything make no sense. You are living as an imagined astronaut—for months on end. Someone has calculated how much oxygen and carbon dioxide you need in your dome. Someone knows how to control the temperature inside your suit, so it feels as though you can survive -255 degrees. Someone has freeze dried your food rations and packed in your water. Your shoes are dusted. You walk a treadmill rigged to give you the sensation of altered gravity.

I'm in a local inn flaking skin off my leg.
I'm on my phone, rating this trip
5 stars.

Stories are social—they serve different purposes for different groups people.

What purpose does Geronimo serve for the settlers of so-nominated Geronimo Springs in Truth or Consequences, New Mexico—and the retirees in San Antonio, Texas?

These so-called Vacancies. The man was captured.
A narrative to reinforce.

I can't get free of my wish to be amorphous to you. I want to spill the same floating signs I get from you and not these bad jokes in my mouth. You going dark on my page. You leaving me alone in the night. What on Earth is it distracting me from?

How we've barely met.

Because there is no chance of reply, I perhaps feel you're the only one who will listen.

In 1995, a group of Believers called Heaven's Gate moved to the area near Truth or Consequences, New Mexico. In 1997, as part of its 4,000-year orbit of the sun, the comet Hale–Bopp passed by the Earth.

During the early 1990s, Heaven's Gate began heavily recruiting members.

Led by a charismatic music professor, the group abandoned their families of origin and earthly possessions and moved, first to Colorado, and then New Mexico, under the belief that extraterrestrial spacecraft would soon descend and take them to a Kingdom of Heaven. The group prepared, learning, studying and waiting. They remained celibate for years.

When the comet Hale–Bopp passed at its closest distance to the Earth, Heaven's Gate took the sign. They drank a lethal mixture of alcohol and toxins and completed a mass suicide. 39 people lay down to enter their alien spacecraft.

This is *disaster, bad star*.

Or some kind of bizarre consequence, remnants of social life in a land rife with conflict and suppressed colonial history. A kind of group pathology or exit.

A star eating itself to supernova. A colonial joke.

On Mars, you walk and walk and walk on your treadmill and tell yourself you're moving forward. You walk and walk and walk on your treadmill. But there is a door back to Earth.

You could, you could, you could, walk outside.

I do want a love that is fundamentally inhabitable. I want more art, I think, though I am writing of what our distance produces. But I want it all. *And I want it at no further cost.* On the other side of the phrase: *I live on Mars*, there is one hand in the audience asking, *But why?*

You taught me how to see from out there. You lent me the vantage to see myself from space. Your glasses were tinted with stars and your bolo tie, Mercury. And now, I think I see the exit door to Earth. I tell myself, I should take it.

The night falls and the novelist leaves his lover at shore. Disease spreads, and the evening apocalypses as under the passage of a perennial celestial object, *Kometen*. I drink orange juice from the carton and turn the heat high, pay with a restlessness of night sweats. Little beads of salt on my eyebrow, and I hope you feel as free, briefly, as I do briefly.

Free breakfast at 7:30 am tomorrow, enough time to load up for my tour of the Spaceport.

In "The Comet Song," Björk sings, *With our fingers we make a million holes.*

I fly to the Kármán line
I determine it's a lie
capital flows
across boundaries
labor does it
in secret

Here a toothbrush
caught at the border
The Kármán line

may well floss teeth

exosphere.

thermosphere.

mesosphere.

stratosphere.

troposphere.

The WIPP (Waste Isolation Pilot Project) in Carlsbad
is supposedly the ideal Earth environment
to store nuclear waste

The cave is 2,150 feet below ground
Someone proposes space

Zach Valdez texts me a series of msgs:
   omg
   on french radio just now
   this man in his space ship, i no longer
   remember what its called
   radio host: x-space
   a oui oui, x-space

I was in a middle seat enveloped by the warm outer
thighs of women

I was wanting to retweet @anne_boyer:

   it wld seem to me that every book is a lie unless it
   begins by explaining that it exists in a version of the
   world in which 105,000,000,000 dollars are in the
   hands of jeff bezos

In which we take off into a blank blue origin

In which private citizens will bypass my airplane
on the way to space

In which the low-earth orbit is filled with trash

In which a line between futurist and colonist
fantasy is drawn

Am I, was I, wanting? I'm saving my paychecks

I smoked in space and space was my dream
I learned the intro and watched the films
Twisted the language, created a fresh batch

I read the internet

Ate my words

With payment totaling 250,000, I'm sure
we can recommend something

With payment totaling 500,000,000, I'm sure
we can recommend something

I made my bed with the @astropoets who warned:

> Week of 12/14 in Pisces: Sometimes you are
> genuinely surprised, but most of the time, you know
> what was going to happen. So no excuses really.
> When they say bring out the roses, take one and give
> thanks to the moon from months ago who made this
> certain rose.

You knew?

I believe I can claim to have known

I knew in the way that doubt is embedded in all
beliefs, the way Wittgenstein said, *if you know
that here is one hand, we'll grant you all the rest*

I have an email signature I delete when writing
personal emails

I hate my own sell-sword ways

Let's say I am first an ecology

Let's say like any Martian I inhabit space

Let's say my weapon is my geosemiotic radar

Or barring that let's say I was in the drawing room
with the wrench

I followed someone on Instagram
and they started dying in front of my eyes

I'm dying here too, but not as fast

I'm full with these little insights, still my questions pile up

      how do you do?

I comment on Alexander Wang
                  boots
                  on your feed

    you could be phenomenal
    you could be a golden eagle

I wrote and performed a play of gendered names like
Iris and Daisy. Gems, beads, Crystal, Ruby

A document titled "fantasies of reproductive failure"

Can you trace an imperial loophole?
    like dark matter

        you helped me and healed me and shared
        energy with me in close proximity and from
        your own distant spaces with your own
        spirit and intelligences you were there with
        me when I suffered and you knew

            Reproduce a rock
            Reproduce a tree
            Reproduce a lake

What the Boundary

A particle, even an association can flash into being, dissolve, then flash over there.[18]

I might've described our separation in terms of star death. You might've said my address was never directional. Barthes writes of ravishment, *ravissement*. I don't know where to go from here, having disembarked again. I sit at this threshold of change with a desire to be unknown.

The sky this far south is less hazy with smoke from smoldering northern forest fires. Still, I think about contaminants.

aaronseyer: The real "Rocket Man"!
levarforever: I'm so sad I missed the live stream
haljordan70: That's great can't wait till there is a manned mission
andyglatfelter: They said it couldn't be done. Now 10x!!!!!!!!
multipole: Soon it'll be hundreds, and then thousands
caindacosta: i want to get away i want to fly away
realjdcope: The future is here!

The US Government's Office of Nuclear Energy at present lists three reasons why we don't launch nuclear waste into space.

1. It's very expensive
2. Space is complicated
3. Rockets are not perfect

Finally:

> *It is not worth risking rocket failures when we already have safe and secure ways to store spent nuclear fuel right here on Earth.*

In 1978, NASA published a technical paper titled *Nuclear Waste Disposal in Space*. The paper begins, *The disposal of certain components of high level nuclear waste in space appears to be feasible from a technical standpoint.*

The paper goes on to clarify that disposal of all high-level waste is, in fact, *impractical* because of the high rocket launch rate required and the resulting economic and environmental factors. A separation of waste product, specifically *unused uranium and cladding*, might make storage of waste feasible on the surface of the moon or in solar orbit.

Remote mining techniques could be employed to recover the waste from the lunar surface.[19]

In her study *Wastelanding: Legacies of Uranium Mining in Navajo Country*, Traci Brynne Voyles writes about indigenous and rural working-class communities who have borne the burden of nuclear weapons development in the southwestern US, starting when the US Army began mining plutonium and uranium for use in atomic weaponry during WWII, and continuing with the present-day burial of transuranic nuclear waste in rural, *wastelanded* regions of the southwest.

waste (adj.) 1300, of land, "desolate, uncultivated," from the Anglo-French and Old North French *waste* (Old French *gaste*), or from Latin *vastus* "empty, desolate."

Masahide Koto writes, the *primary targets [of nuclear warfare] ... have been invariably the sovereign nations of Fourth World and indigenous peoples.* She lists nuclear warfare sites, most coded as *tests*—the start-to-finish detonation of nuclear weapons in the world.

Marshall Islands: 66 times
French Polynesia: 175 times
Australian Aborigines: 9 times
Newe Sogobia (the Western Shoshone Nation): 814 times
Christmas Island: 24 times
Hawaii (Kalama Island, also known as Johnston Island):
12 times
Republic of Kazakhstan: 467 times
Uighur (Xinjian Province, China): 36 times[20]

Trinity, New Mexico

Radiation knows no semantics, and contagion knows no
rhetoric. The military deployment of weapons, whether
labeled *test* or *strike*, has all the effects and conditions of
warfare unleashed upon the land and peoples it touches.

Water from the well tapped at my grandparents' land
has been found to contain uranium at four times the
volume recommended by the health department for safe
consumption. We arrive at thresholds, look at patterns,
wonder about safety. My mom gets cancer. It's probably from
something else.

Familiarity breeds this nervous system.[21]

On January 29, 1951, Geiger counters at the Eastman Kodak
Company's film production plant at Lake Ontario detected
high levels of radiation as snow fell around the city. Six
years earlier, just after the July 16, 1945, detonation of the
first atomic weapon, known as the Trinity Test, Kodak
experienced significant financial loss after receiving reports
that their film rolls were coming out cloudy.

The company registered a complaint with the National Association of Photographic Managers, who telegrammed the Atomic Energy Commission. *Tests snowfall Rochester Monday by Eastman. Kodak Company give ten thousand counts per minute, whereas equal volume snow falling previous Friday gave only four hundred. Situation serious. Will report any further results obtained. What are you doing?*

The Atomic Energy Commission released a statement to the press. *Investigating reports that snow fell in Rochester was measurably radioactive.*

My mom's uterine cancer requires internal radiation. I touch her back as she hears this at the doctor's office. The problem, she tries to explain, is that she knows too much.

I look into calculating my annual radiation dose on a typical year, an idea I get from the US Nuclear Regulatory Commission. The tab says *Radiation is All Around Us.*

It's a strange body feeling to attune oneself to a number.

It seems we live in a radioactive world, that radiation has always been constitutive of our material surroundings. I calculate my cosmic radiation, from outer space, which at sea level is only 26 mrem. At 7,000 feet where I live, this number is between 40 and 50 mrem. I calculate my terrestrial radiation from the ground. A state bordering the Gulf or Pacific coast is exposed to 23 mrem. The Colorado Plateau area around Denver is exposed to 90 mrem. Everywhere else clocks in around 43 mrem.

If you live in a stone, brick or concrete building, add 7 mrem.

If you eat food and drink water, add 40 mrem.

If you breathe the (radon in the) air, add 200 mrem.

If you travel by jet plane, have porcelain crowns, wear a luminous wristwatch, use luggage inspection at the airport, watch TV, have a smoke detector, wear a plutonium-powered cardiac pacemaker, live within 50 miles of a nuclear power plant, or live within 50 miles of a coal-fired electrical utility plant, add more mrem. I do my best, and come out with 410.01 mrem, a number I have no emotional relationship to. This calculation feels like it betrays me, like everything I've heard about radiation's destructive potential is wrong. *Radiation is All Around Us.*

According to the chart, natural radiation sources account for about 82 percent of all public radiation exposure. Manmade radiation sources account for the remaining 18 percent *for a typical person.*

Executives at the Kodak Company, after their complaint following the secret detonation of a 1-kiloton nuclear device, code name Able, at the Nevada Proving Ground, were granted "Q" clearances to receive information in advance of atomic tests to alter plant operations and protect film merchandise, so the company could secure profit margins despite radioactive fallout.

K O D A K (1892)
You Press the Button, We Do the Rest!

Communities living downwind of the nuclear test sites were never given warning.

The atomic story is one of tapping into, and harnessing, a destructive universal force of radiation, of matter's self-immolating potentiality on Earth. The story goes, we've mastered it. But there is only story, itself a drive, and the inevitable unleashing of force, a narrative entropy that unspools in place.

The occupational exposure limit for radiation is 5,500 mrem per year. An occupational dose of 1,000 mrem increases the chance of eventually developing a fatal cancer.

The detonation of atomic weapons and the mining of heavy metals for their production is a known cause of harm for humans and *various ecological receptors*.

Radiation is all around us. One story betrays another.

Two Westerns

Open Range
Dead Man

High Noon
A Fistful of Dollars

A Bullet for the General
For a Few Dollars More

Dawn Must Always Recur
Four Guns to the Border

The Wind and Beyond

A tour at Spaceport America offers visitors an opportunity to explore and learn about the world's first purpose-built commercial spaceport located in New Mexico, USA. Here is a general overview of what you might expect on a tour at Spaceport America:

1. Visitor Center: The tour typically begins at the Visitor Center, where you may check in, receive an orientation, and learn about the history and significance of Spaceport America. The Visitor Center often features interactive exhibits, displays, and educational materials related to space exploration and the commercial space industry.

2. Facility Tour: The tour proceeds with a guided visit to various facilities within Spaceport America. This may include:

   Terminal Hangar Facility: You may have the opportunity to see the state-of-the-art facility where space tourists and astronauts will depart from. This hangar is designed to accommodate the launch vehicles and spacecraft used for commercial spaceflights.

   Operations Center: Visitors might have a chance to visit the Operations Center, which serves as the nerve center for coordinating space missions, flight operations, and ground support activities.

   Vertical Launch Area: You may have a glimpse of the vertical launch area, where rockets and launch vehicles are prepared and launched into space. The tour guide might explain the launch procedures and safety measures involved.

Mission Control: Some tours may provide access to the Mission Control Center, where teams monitor and control spaceflights and ensure the safety and success of each mission.

3. Outdoor Sites: Depending on the tour, there might be opportunities to explore outdoor sites around Spaceport America. This could include viewing areas where you can witness the expansive runways, launch pads, or the surrounding desert landscape.

4. Educational Presentations: Throughout the tour, you might have the chance to attend educational presentations or talks by space industry experts, sharing insights into the commercial space industry, space tourism, and the future of space exploration.

It's important to note that the specific details of the tour, including the areas visited and activities offered, may vary depending on the tour operator and the availability of certain areas within the spaceport. It's recommended to check with the official Spaceport America website or contact the tour operator for the most accurate and up-to-date information about the tour experience.

A girl walks into a bar full of promise
and I am up here *I embarrass myself*

Wanting to be rich and shitty
we have to present ourselves

In real and imagined autobiography
when you find yourself amplifying

When crushed and guilty, then more
phantasy like a cherry

Like you were so hard
being wrong when even

Reversing the direction
an intellectual friendship

If you were to uplift one thing
at the expense of others

Oneself
I have found friends

Among the artists
I have been waiting my whole life

To say in front of everyone
I have been institutionally blessed

I thank you for the opportunity
to examine space

An invocation to try
an irritation under the nail

No one wants you to admit
how you were crushed

How you couldn't help
your own condition

It's only
natural if you're zero

And I own
what I wanted after all

To say queer
is just to say every

unsaid thing

Spaceport America

I approach the Spaceport terminal. I can barely hear the radio over my Ford's air conditioning. There's nothing out here but sun.

The terminal building is constructed like an eye viewed from space. An elongated pupil, with the building's apron completing the iris. From the road, like a lump in an endless horizon, the Spaceport's soft organic form is a subtle dysregulation in the landscape.

I park, approach.

Weightlessness, also known as zero gravity, is an experience of *free fall*, which occurs when gravity is the only force acting on a mass, as in an astronaut's experience of space. Gravity still acts upon the astronaut, in space as on Earth, but without air molecules and supportive surfaces, astronauts do not perceive its effects.

Visitors and astronauts gain access to Spaceport America's facilities through a sunken channel carved into the terrain. The channel's walls serve as an exhibition area, showcasing a history of space exploration intertwined with a narrative of the region and its settlers. The channel's linear design extends seamlessly into the building, leading to a mezzanine level overlooking an expansive super hangar. This is where the spacecraft and the simulation room are housed.

This tour is hard to land. It's at weird times, by request, with persistence, through endlessly ringing phones and dial tones.

Are you a journalist? No. Click.

Are you a journalist? Yes. Ok. What's your number?

A small group of people gathers in the front of the building, then snakes around our peppy guide.

The Spaceport's terminal building is connected to the hangar, which, as I recall, is a large enclosed structure designed to house and protect aircraft, spacecraft, and other large vehicles. The terminal building, for people, features a glass window facing a runway. This building provides a vantage point for observing the departure of spacecraft, almost as if the show is as important as the launch.

The guide describes this as a coveted viewing platform.

The position occupied by the speaker who—

We snap photos of empty concrete.

The architecture of the terminal building is supposed to take advantage of the topography of the surrounding land. Embedded in the earth, the terminal uses thermal mass, the building's ability to absorb, store, and release heat, to regulate internal temperatures and insulate against harsh weather. The hottest temperature on record here was recorded recently. 107°F.

Our tour guide points out a coffee bar in the center of the terminal, the spaceport's *social hub*. The café's tables are snuggled in together and ringed by low-seated cream white chairs. I do like coffee. (The café is closed.)

The 568th human in space, a Virgin Galactic Pilot, was just awarded his Commercial Astronaut Wings by the US Department of Transportation. He flew Virgin Galactic's SpaceShipTwo, which launched from Spaceport America.

It was not as loud as I thought it would be, and the motor was a lot smoother than I thought it would be. But the acceleration is pretty eye watering and its pretty instantaneous. It feels like a catapult shot.

The first SpaceShipTwo vehicle, VSS Enterprise, crashed in a flight. This was a setback. Despite this breakup, the company has adjusted and will soon launch commercial flights, a moment it has been anticipating for years.

Our guide leads us into the main building, where a mural covers most of the wall. *The Journey Upward* begins on the far side of the room with depictions of ancient people observing the stars. It concludes with an illustration of a conceptual Aerospace Hotel. The remarkable *Journey*, spanning countless millennia, culminates in people circling the Earth at a luxury hotel. I picture tourists snapping photos at liftoff from circular windows and remember that only last year, four private passengers paid $55 million to spend two weeks on the International Space Station.

I think, maps all have the same cartographic ethos: a desire for narrative order.

In 1966, a treaty called the Outer Space Treaty was proposed and opened for signature a year later by three depository governments: the Russian Federation, the United Kingdom and the United States of America. The nation signatories, at the time, agreed to principles concerning the use of and access to outer space, providing the basic framework for international space law:

1. The exploration and use of outer space shall be carried out for the benefit and in the interests of all countries and shall be the province of all mankind;
2. Outer space shall be free for exploration and use by all States;
3. Outer space is not subject to national appropriation by claim of sovereignty, by means of use or occupation, or by any other means;
4. States shall not place nuclear weapons or other weapons of mass destruction in orbit or on celestial bodies or station them in outer space in any other manner;
5. The Moon and other celestial bodies shall be used exclusively for peaceful purposes;
6. Astronauts shall be regarded as the envoys of mankind;
7. States shall be responsible for national space activities whether carried out by governmental or non-governmental entities;
8. States shall be liable for damage caused by their space objects; and
9. States shall avoid harmful contamination of space and celestial bodies.[22]

Alsace-Lorraine, where France has long pursued the acquisition and safeguarding of what it perceived as its *inherent frontier*—the Pyrenees in the southwest, the Alps in the southeast, and the Rhine River in the northeast—has long been upended in border conflict. The region—the western side of the Rhine River—was annexed by the Roman Empire and later, invaded again by Germany. My French grandfather was carried as a baby out of France by boat, his parents taking with them, illegally and absurdly, their centuries-old grapevines.

But when I think of France, I think of diamonds. *Europe is literally the creation of the third world.*[23]

Layli Long Soldier writes, of agreements made with indigenous peoples in the continuous re-appropriation of lands that became the United States: *As treaties were abrogated (broken) and new treaties were drafted, one after another, the new treaties often referenced old defunct treaties and it is a muddy, switchback trail to follow.*[24] In an epoch of national boundaries, what is a treaty, if not a sovereignty bound to the military enforcement of borders?

Immanently, commercial space travelers will have the chance to cross all kinds of thresholds, as Virgin Galactic prepares for its first private citizen rocket launch:

Passengers aboard VSS Unity [will] experience a roughly 90-minute journey, including a signature air launch and Mach-3 boost to space. They'll enjoy several minutes of out-of-seat weightlessness as they view Earth from the spaceship's 17 windows.

I read a Yelp review at Spaceport America's page:

Just a disappointment from the moment we arrived. The American flag is in tatters, wrapped helplessly, knotted and devoid of the honor it deserves. If you can't fly it correctly, don't fly it at all. (A sign at its base indicates it's being flown in "honor" of an individual citizen.)

EVERY AMERICAN FLAG

I look around.

Here at Spaceport America, along the Jornada del Muerto, part of the Camino Real de Tierra Adentro, the Silver Route, I'm on a 1,590-mile road from Mexico City to Ohkay Owingeh pueblo. The road crosses the US–Mexico border. Already a colonial construction, presently maintained variably, this road cannot be traversed start-to-end without an encounter with the regulatory agency known as Border Control.

Sometimes, these encounters are carceral. Sometimes they are fatal. *Desire to cross a threshold. Fear not to. If you could please work on your boundaries.*

Our tour guide, looking around with raised eyebrows, is talking about the weightlessness of astronauts. Being relieved from the burden of weight on your feet may sound soothing, he is saying. But over time, it leads to health issues. Weakening of bones and muscles, various internal changes. One of the objectives of the International Space Station is to investigate the impact of weightlessness on astronaut well-being.

I peel off from the tour and walk outside across a stretch of dusty pavement. There's something about Spaceport A that pricks me, but it's when I'm looking away from its structure and out, past its compelling architecture, that I really feel something.

My eyes drift up and I think about airspace.

Of lightning, *no continuous path from sky to ground can satisfy its wild imaginings, its insistence on experimenting with different possible ways to connect, playing at all matter of errant wanderings in a virtual exploration of diverse forms of coupling and dis/connected alliance.*[25]

The air above me is full of invisible material and energy. It is full of matter—and memory.

A Spaceport, site of boundless desire for the twenty-first-century tourist, is here transposed upon an existing space. That same air was once called *empty*, its grounds, *wasteland*. It was called *go for launch*, called Test Site, called Ground Zero. The White Sands Missile Range.

It was then called Trinity.

Leonid's Meteor Shower

I would use other words to describe the arc of a mountain, which was just described to me in mathematical terms as a hyperbolic tangent. The mountain emerged on the horizon out of a grey evening wash years ago, when my sister and I were walking with my father, ostensibly to look for deer. We were not to speak on this walk as we were looking for deer.

Were we in fact looking for deer? We were looking to be together without speaking.

I'll take you there. Cool night, light coat, Leonid's meteor shower. (Perhaps we were looking for stars.) Squarely in the arc of the mountain, which is only a distant, curved line, my sister, my father, and I moved against knowing the surround or even each other. Usually, my father absorbs all feelings and remains perfectly still. I absorb all his stillness and remain perfectly still. My sister absorbs all my stillness and remains perfectly still. Like a lake receiving tossed rocks with no ripple, we absorb.

In the history of mathematics, the hyperbolic tangent is a newer mathematical function. (Hyperbolic geometry is a non-Euclidean geometry.) Euclid's propositions, many compiled from theories by early Greek mathematicians, were set out in his infamous *Elements*, a thirteen-book series written in Alexandria around 300 BCE. *Elements* is one of the most influential books ever written, second only to the Bible in the number of editions since its first printing in 1482. For hundreds of years, its proposals were challenged, but were not toppled.

On our walk for deer, the world still and the mountain ahead only linear, I stooped to the ground and playfully grabbed a handful of leaves. As I remember it, a cactus pricked through my glove. My dad, hearing me cry out, turned. A single long spine, an inch or more, was hooked through the fabric and into my flesh. Pulling on it yielded more pain than relief, and it didn't budge.

What's that above the mountain? my dad asked, prompting our distracted glances away. *Shooting star!*

Non-Euclidean geometry altered, forever, western cultural understandings of space. Since its subject was an exhibit of rationality, the Euclidean perspective, as I understand it, represented authority. The shift, demonstrated in new theories, was from that of absolute truth to relative truths about spatial dynamics, a shift in European ways of thinking about knowledge. No longer did it make sense to argue, based on Euclidean postulates, that an unadulterated knowledge of space is an absolute truth.

Was it even? *Satellite.*

Like a dad in a story, my father took the opportunity to reach down and yank the cactus from my hand in one tug, dragging it half an inch, or more in memory, from my hand. I felt the sharp pain of a reverse puncture and relief. Under the mountain, our scene was a sudden coherence of mutually constitutive narratives, and I had my setting, its facility.

In a story, setting provides a background against a foreground of self-making. But here? Setting wants to be foregrounded. People move in and out, antagonists whose moments ebb and flow, but the rest persists. Soon, my narrative will fall away, leaving only the hyperbolic tangent and the sky.

I've been told to *use* setting. But setting is its own self-making. I realize I'll come again and look for deer after dusk, and I'll do so long after my father is gone.

What it takes to speak against claim

soothe a wound
admit its seepage
bend an ear to its
undisciplined
inversions

rumpled composite
of longing and belonging

surface-wet grass
intrinsically dry

Home

The position occupied by the speaker who said nothing
but sat looking out the window.

The position occupied by the speaker who said nothing
but sat looking out the window.

The position occupied by the speaker who said nothing
but sat looking out the window.

The position occupied by the speaker who said nothing
but sat looking out the window.

> Is there a social ill in deboning
> generations of belief
> with one bumper sticker

I peel off hundreds of layers of outerwear like

blouse

and *pant*

exosphere.

thermosphere.

mesosphere.

stratosphere.

troposphere.

Trinity Site

The Trinity Site of the Manhattan Project is on the north
end of 4,000-square-mile White Sands Missile Range outside
Truth or Consequences, New Mexico. Pieces of fused silica
rock formed in the heat of the blast still scatter the ground.

Now, *Women of the West* series playing in Manhattan

Later, Manhattan or Manhattan Project?

In Santa Fe a foam replica of the Trinity Memorial from a
film set. My dad walked me down

    You'll like this

I'm here with these preoccupations

To connect these boroughs
as it takes time at all (out

of time) to link Queens
New York to Truth

or Consequences, I
guess 2nd Street

took the L train east
ended up at Primo

Auto Parts

Meanwhile, everyone
knows that West is
Cardinal direction

So is Woman
for that matter I
buy a can of soda

Primo is in Ridgewood, Queens, off the Halsey stop on the L.
The auto shop is a thriving business, one of several mechanic
shops on this radioactive site, which once produced thorium
for the Atomic Energy Commission

I've consumed all the sugar
my blood can currently handle

*Westward the Women. The Ballad of Little Jo. Bullets for Breakfast.
Thomasine and Bushrod. Hellfire. Arizona. Cattle Queen of
Montana. The Belle Star Story. Rita of the West. The Shooting.
Meeks Cutoff*

My great-aunts were cowgirls. I learned how to ride a horse.
A horse stepped on my sister's foot.

I watch her best shot
in a dark theater

The Wolff-Alport Site:

In 1923 a chemical engineer named Harry Wolff founded a chemical laboratory with his business partner Max Alport in Ridgewood, Queens

In 1947 the Atomic Energy Commission started buying thorium from Wolff-Alport

In 1955 an atomic weapon of uranium-233 derived from thorium was tested in Nevada

Where the curb of the street
crumbles chalk on my
shoe it's fall I know this

Route sunny, the Superfund
I've read in
the papers

In 2014, the E.P.A. assigned Superfund status to the former
Wolff-Alport lab in Queens, New York. They'd already
installed concrete, lead, and steel protections under boards
and sidewalks to block radiation

*But the agency's goal, he said, is to ensure that the site can be used in
the future*

Perhaps even for residential
development a white blanketing

The E.P.A. calls
Primo Auto Parts

A dilapidated
warehouse

A thriving business
to clean up

And the bodega
where I bought

Poetry you're not representing yourself
it's very small this town

Being Founded up a school uniform like up
you, up yours in French or Spanish

Or this project of reinvention
innovating us out of existence

This bright can
humid nodding

What do you do to flee
the Enchantment

The Kármán Line

The Kármán line is the international boundary between the Earth and space. Due to inconsistencies in the Earth's atmosphere this border is approximate. It marks the end of national boundaries and the beginning of what is known as

free space

I'm looking at a photograph of space company headquarters. I see a little girl at seven years old. She wears twisted pigtails, blue Nikes, and a space suit fitted just for her. She's holding a kid-sized space helmet and looking down in thought. She's blonde and blue-eyed. I'm in bed pondering lonely questions. What does the poetic form make available that's not available by other means? I ask you silently without words. Without asking I wish for someone to know how to receive me and my questions. *Does the past remain with us as friend? As foe?*

The Kármán line describes the human capacity for airborne activity. This limit is changing quickly as our means of access to the outer layers of the atmosphere and space alter, faster than I can write, faster than I can pace out this long wail.

I'd like to describe a lifetime of erotic injury and repair. I'd like to describe a juice fast, carb fast, titration curve. I look at the cat playing with flickering afternoon light on the wall and I know the cat knows these are the good times. Other times we stand back across the room and hope we see the room blink.

Debates about globalization over the course of the last four decades have grappled with an increasing sense of the diminished sovereignty of nation-states, while historical studies of nationalism and nations have similarly highlighted the ways in which the political, economic, and cultural forms of society are porous and contingent. Nevertheless, as contemporary conflicts over immigration reveal with particular intensity, popular investments in the modular nation form and claims to a discrete and territorially delimited political community have definite material force.[26]

The Kármán line circumscribes the simply global orientation that has been a limit on human activity, if not on the imaginary. It's an asymptotal curb on fantasies of its perforation. We hold the border hard fantasizing about what it looks, feels, and tastes like to cross. We don't ask for consent for there's seemingly no one to ask. We don't negotiate terms because we invented this language. I note what's been named, defined and militarized, what reassures in its delineation of national boundaries, fictions that for the moment make nation-states seem an inevitability.

The leaves are quivering outside. I knew fewer trees in New York City than I ever did where I grew up. Is that what signals home, where you know the trees? You point out the trees that don't belong in the Southwest. Cottonwood trees I associate with watering holes and tire swings gleaming with wet skin and a queer loneliness, invasive species. I think about loving a wrong tree, an invasive tree, its luxuriating spread a reminder of seeds scattered without attention to the disorder the land wanted, how it's our problem now to love.

Circumstances introduced me to life in a land I didn't at first belong. Belonging may be a sense of earned integration. Belonging is probably intra-acting agencies. It may be socially constructed, relational phenomena that account for identity and relationship—but these are built, torn down, and rebuilt every day. *Of course I exist due to variable aural levels. In this sense my presence is unfiltered, primeval, dispossessed of quotidian numeration, no longer prone to biography as a warren.*[27]

In fact, the line between earth and space is a riot. And a rocket manifests its power over and through. To concern yourself in *this place* with the health, wellbeing, and sustenance of life and not-life in *this place* and to ask of the integrated and delicate network some permission to percolate into *this place* may be to admit first that some forms of contact will leave a scar. It's both simple and too much to admit to this kind of impression, to its prevalence.

Some days, if I can believe it, I even walk up and down Fifth Avenue. I see networks of endlessly interconnected interests protecting property, development, and nuclear production. I feel like explaining to my students that my childhood plays in my mind. In faded color, I see myself rewinding.

Sometimes when I say *space* I mean stars. Sometimes I mean what has been made surplus or treated as resource, what relies on the rendering of space empty or *elsewhere*. I point to this, but I wish, far beyond pointing, to make a space that resists both this narrative of containment and its diagnosis. *Resource* vs. *empty*, *inside* vs. *outside*, *you* vs. *me*: fantasies distributed by armed vehicles.

Like Espolòn in my veins, writing dilates its containers. *Finding "the one" in a sea of dirty DMs.* If desire is the projection of oneself outside oneself, that and our dirty mingling show the lie that is our story of self-containment. I expand, contract, pollute. I check my DMs in the morning.

Against his observation that *the ego seems to maintain clear and sharp lines of demarcation,* Freud uses the example of lovers, a state of consciousness in which the boundaries between the ego and the object erode. *Against all the evidence of his senses, a man who is in love declares that "I" and "you" are one, and is prepared to behave as if it were a fact.*[28] What remains after ego erosion?

I write in space, a kind of ongoing self-transgression determined by wind and seed, fingertip, bath, multiple simultaneous touch, in sickness and health and textual pollution. Like a meteor shower, *I fall strait down like rain.*[29] I meet the match for my desire to pulverize the acquired thing. I vomit letters and you suck them up. The phonemes become matted silences you call out while I touch you and retreat, come again, and retreat.

You might sit under a tree not knowing some trees filtering sun are foreign invaders. Nothing here is as it was. Everything is some fruit grafted to some other fruit.

The Kármán line is a gradation, and there's a multitude of feeling beyond.

Arthur Sze writes, *I swing out of myself on invisible wings.*

Meltdown

I wanted to hear the kind of noise a living thing makes.[30]

As I disband from my group viewing Spaceport America's facilities, my mind fogs and memory overtakes the lingering voice of the tour guide mumbling about recycled rockets.

Perhaps I didn't want to see Spaceport America as much as its predecessor, an empty field and sky behind barbed wire and foreboding signs. This or that rocket launch is framed by an airspace, a manscaped aerial garden of missile testing, a heady nuclear project resulting in proliferation of nonsense deterrence.

Or perhaps I wished to see this airspace to understand something else.

In *From Trinity to Trinity*, Kyoko Hayashi writes about the arms factory where she was working as a junior high student during the atomic bombing at the Mitsubishi shipyard in Nagasaki on August 9, 1945. When she, unthinkably, survives this event, Hayashi undertakes a journey to Trinity, New Mexico, site of the first-ever atomic bomb detonation. Her pilgrimage, 54 years after the war, is more than a physical journey to a place of origin and death. She collapses time and space.

When I was a child, I dreamed of rockets. Playing in a dusty field by an empty volleyball court, I mimicked liftoff. At the time, I was living and attending elementary school in Shiprock, New Mexico, not far from a rural town called Church Rock.

About ten years before I was born, this small town was the site of the largest radioactive spill in US history.

On July 16, 1979, over eleven hundred tons of acidic, radioactive tailings solution poured into the Puerco River near Church Rock, New Mexico, spilling an estimated 1.36 short tons of uranium and 46 curies of alpha contaminants downstream across 80 miles onto the Navajo Nation. The United Nuclear Corporation, which operated a uranium mill bordering Navajo Tribal Trust lands, was responsible for the breach of its disposal area for radioactive waste.

The Church Rock nuclear spill received less media coverage than Three Mile Island, despite its larger-scale impact of radiation sickness, cancers, and deaths.

Kyoko Hayashi's visit to Trinity fuses dislocated times and places. In lyric prose translated into English by dancer Eiko Otake, Hayashi writes that her arrival to Trinity ushers a sense of being tethered to two colonial forces. A citizen of Japan, and the mother of children who are US citizens, she criticizes the idea of the sovereign, bounded nation from the perspective of a *hibakusha*, an atomic bomb survivor.

While driving on a white road that seemed to extend far into the distance, I had a strong sensation of realizing that I was on the same land that contains the atomic bomb test site. I have to go, I decided without any hesitation. If I can make that journey, I can hold August 9 within my life circle. If I can never be free from the event, I should end my relationship by swallowing it.[31]

Hayashi's orientation to New Mexico is a narrative always re-writing itself, one that inevitably contains the past and the present, the before and the after. This circularity makes a moment of overlay, where time and space collapse, like a snake's mouth on its own tail.

Description of timeline: which came first
Description of site: what placed where

The Church Rock nuclear spill is a legacy of the atomic project initiated at Trinity. Where once bloomed extenuated disaster, a nearby desert, forever linked to this ground zero, fractured under uranium extraction and its casualties. So we fragment and cohere again, like collective memory.

Still at the Spaceport launchpad, I look out over a landscape once construed as *empty*. The feeling is familiar enough, the narrative is almost easy to digest—though the air feels full and known, for example, even to me, in body knowledge with some relation to early memory. Late summer smells, a collision of dirt, water, and ozone, thunderstorms. Flashes of unscripted images. School, grandparents, lovers.

I look out. Is this what I wanted to see?
(There is no close reading.)
Spaceport America: you are standing very still.

Elizabeth Povinelli argues, *to wish for a redemptive narrative, to seek it, is to wish that social experiments fulfill rather than upset given conditions, that they emerge in a form that given conditions recognize as good, and that they comply to a hegemony of love rather than truly challenge its hold over social life.*

I know it's all related—absentia, craving, denial, Chipotle at night, Spaceport America in our dreams, this bereavement.

Hundreds of years of rupture and loss in every window display.

Sites of empire speak to each other, whisper stories in my ear. *Trinity* is here and elsewhere, accessible only in fragments. Across these fragments, a breach, where suturing breach may not be feasible. I wish for the kind of knowing that involves sitting in the knowledge of breach, dissolving attachments to self, unbreached. There is violence in this, or potential for it. There is also relief.

Invited to paint a mural for hotel guests in a room at the Albuquerque hotel Nativo Lodge, artist Marina Eskeets, from Naná'áztiin, New Mexico (The Big Curve, NM, Navajo Nation), paints sunflowers: *Phytoremediation in the Glittering World*. She writes:

Sunflowers are unique plants, known as hyperaccumulators because of their ability to grow and capture contaminates in soil and ground water. Their roots reach down into the earth and pull toxicities from beneath and store them in their roots, stems, and leaves. The process is known as phytoremediation when used to clean areas affected by radiation contamination...

Pull down the roses, no
Pull down some late fall flower
Hold on, this season is going to last

I'm here, at Spaceport America, but I'm also there, at the other launch. The detonation event that eerily conditions my own story's silences.

Or perhaps it isn't that launch. Not the event, but events prior to the event. Not the bomb, but its production, not the flash but its long history of material extraction and grief, which has conditioned the structuring of my and our relations, our lack of porousness, our memory: nation, state, people.

I want to deal with this history, my exposure to it.

Back at the hotel in Truth or Consequences, it's 105 degrees.

Is it a meeting
or is it exposure therapy

Is it a meeting
or is it a sentence

Is it a meeting
or is it a soap box

Is it a meeting
or is it holy and free futures

Is it a meeting
or is it these birds of paradise

Is it a meeting
or did I leave something unsaid

Is it a meeting
or is it my full disclosure

Is it a meeting
or were we too far gone

Is it a meeting
or can't you smoke in here

Is it a meeting
or is it my silences

Is it a meeting
or is it the turn away

Or is it some kind of dance
is it a party

Or is it free and unholy
futures

I split the difference measured
17 mins the express going local

Against 17 mins wait
for the express

Either way does the work of
is it a meeting

Or am I crazy
did I see some kind of light

Is it a meeting
did we meet another time I can't

Remember the difference
between knowing and

Seeing you from a distance
measure the gaps in my

Refusals every time
I put one foot in front

I lost time
I see it differently now

Injured? Later they walked
met with no consequence

While the whole world watched
and waited

And spoke against waiting
the sun set

And it was later
I trudged through cold and flu season

Covered my nose and mouth
I washed my hands often

With soap and water
how we assign blame

How we don't

Hi.

I'm writing this instead of writing you back.

I walk up the street. In downtown over the tracks where there's coffee, up and back around the hill. I think about knowing, a practice we've capitalized ("K" = !) and imbue with a weight that distributes in hierarchy. (! = Knowing better, Knowing about, "K.")

I write instead of reaching out. I recognize there's no contact without touch, no immersion without enfolding live presence like ammo in these arms. I delete the apps, delete maps, place two feet for one minute outside on hot pavement. I ask where rupture happens, from the inside out, the outside in, or the outside out.

I pack the car.

Leaving my hotel in Truth or Consequences, I take off at dawn to beat the heat. Something has lifted. I know I will still feel the parts of myself I've left behind, but the radio commands me, don't remain in the past like a ghost haunting a singular site of excavation. Bring your experiences far forward and deeply backwards into the complexity that's here.

As I squint into this story, I can't help but associate my visit with a rush of feeling. And while feeling isn't primary, it's here. There's poetry. How it provokes an eroding self to burst open like a late-stage star. There's conversation with the world in a mutually permeable nearness, even if matter's distances can't always be measured as inseparable from the unruly activities of our lives.

Robert Morris calls duration *the present tense of immediate spatial experience, just the present.*

Years from now, back in Albuquerque, I will watch a live video of speakers commemorating the 75th anniversary of the Trinity Test. The same day, an op-ed in the *New York Times* will worry over a proposal to bring back nuclear weapons testing. The following year, an international company will begin exploratory drilling to assess bringing back uranium mining in Church Rock.

On the drive back, I notice the sun peaking from behind a large water tower planting rays across old tread.

Returning to Albuquerque, I know the present contains all of history. Our present-tense language contains all our tears.

I get a drink at the bar, Saints and Sinners. Or I have a drink with you now across time.

Our glasses touch. We say goodbye.

epilogue.

Orbital Economy

In 1768 the Captain James Cook sailed towards
the Pacific islands of Tahiti and Australia

And if I had to describe a spaceport I'd say it's a
wishing well. I'd guess at your departure

A spaceport is a transit site of Kashmir white granite
bathrooms with a line then you leave the Earth

There's a debate as to the exact *colonial contrivance* that
caused the Captain James Cook to sail his bottomless

Some scholars say it was the desire to observe
the transit of Venus across the face of the sun

Was it the transit of Venus threaded that white hot
granite with desire for mastery of the thing. Look

The dry ocean bed has stories it could tell
in a hundred thousand lines *Out of order*

The ship was called the good ship Endeavor intended
to find a southern continent mapping space

I have seen your locked lips and come home sweating I
write on my wall if you'll notice. Waiting

In interstitial spaces in this story I said
a slice of blue is a dawn in any distance

I can feel the rain holding me in a captivity
I truly wanted in this house to read and think

It's a rainy day fund we're using here but
we're starting to develop a poetics of

And did you want to join me for dinner? Back-
channeling did you want to pay for this now?

Our assembly of the dissimilar, now a grave
At the Poetry Project I read *Effaced from her meek*

Brow all lines of sickness grief and care what we
left as we moved across the sky

notes

1 "She will reach the Kármán line": *The Kármán Line*, directed by Oscar Sharpe, 2014

2 "Je bâtis a roches mon langage": Édouard Glissant, *Poetics of Relation*

3 "P.S.: more than anything": Hervé Guibert, *Mausoleum of Lovers*

4 "Some say the soul is mixed in with the whole universe": Aristotle, *A Presocratics Reader: Selected Fragments and Testimonia*

5 "A card table in the library stands ready": James Merrill, "Lost in Translation"

6 "No one wants to be a bad or compromised kind of force": Lauren Berlant, "Affect Is the New Trauma"

7 "Mode of governance against memory": Rebecca Schneider, *Performing Remains*

8 "For decades the Los Alamos National Laboratory": George Johnson, "Ideas & Trends: Chaos Theory; Harness Fire? Mother Nature Begs to Differ," *The New York Times, May 21, 2000* https://www.nytimes.com/2000/05/21/weekinreview/ideas-trends-chaos-theory-harness-fire-mother-nature-begs-to-differ.html

9 "Lightning is a reaching toward": Karen Barad, "TransMaterialities, Trans*/Matter/Realities and Queer Political Imaginings," *GLQ* 21, no. 2–3 (2015): 387

10 "EVERY AMERICAN FLAG": Demian DinéYazhí´, *my ancestors will not let me forget this*, 2019. Glass, neon, aluminum frame. 42 x 22 x 23 in, displayed in the Hub at the 2019 Honolulu Biennial

11 "You've seen it": Michael Hainey, "Postcards from the Astronauts' Lounge," *Wired*, 2016

12 "What makes us think that matter is lifeless": Karen Barad, 389

13 Baby your song...

14 "Imaginaries of some spaces as *wastelands* are prevalent in the national narratives of colonial nations": Traci Brynne Voyles, *Wastelanding: Legacies of Uranium Mining in Navajo Country*

15 "Vital territory, where nuclear tests might be conducted": Roxanne Panchasi, "'No Hiroshima in Africa': The Algerian War and the Question of French Nuclear Tests in the Sahara," *History of the Present* 9, no. 1 (2019): 84–112

16 "Es freue sich": Brecht?

17 "As the plane banked over urban sprawl": Porter Swetzell

18 "A particle, even an association can flash": Mei-mei Berssenbrugge, *A Treatise on Stars*

19 "Remote mining techniques": R. E. Burns, W. E. Causey, W. E. Galloway, and R. W. Nelson, "NASA Technical Paper 1225: Nuclear Waste Disposal in Space," Scientific and Technical Information Office, 1978

20 "Nuclear warfare sites, most coded as tests": Masahide Kato, "Nuclear Globalism: Traversing Rockets, Satellites, and Nuclear War via the Strategic Gaze," *Alternatives* 18, no. 3 (1993): 348

21 "Familiarity breeds this nervous system": Elizabeth Povinelli

22 "Treaty on Principles Governing the Activities of States in the Exploration and Use of Outer Space, including the Moon and Other Celestial Bodies," United Nations Office for Outer Space Affairs

23 "Europe is literally the creation of the third world": *Concerning Violence*, film by Göran Hugo Olsson, 2023

24 "As treaties were abrogated (broken)," Layli Long Soldier, *Whereas*

25 "No continuous path from sky to ground": Karen Barad, 387

26 "Debates about globalization": Alyosha Goldstein, "Toward a Genealogy of the U.S. Colonial Present," *Formations of United States Colonialism*, 2014

27 "Of course I exist": Will Alexander, *Above the Human Nerve Domain*, 67

28 "Against all evidence of his senses": Sigmund Freud, *Civilization and Its Discontents*

29 "I fall strait down like rain": Harry Dodge, *My Meteorite*

30 "I wanted to hear the kind of noise a living thing makes": Kyoko Hayashi, *From Trinity to Trinity*

31 "While driving on a white road": Kyoko Hayashi, II

acknowledgments

The Kármán Line was written from 2018 to 2023 between NYC and Albuquerque, NM.

Deep thanks to Alyssa Perry, Caryl Pagel, Sevy Perez, and the whole Rescue Press team who took a chance on *The Kármán Line* and believed in its many iterations.

I'm grateful to the editors and publishers who released early versions of the poems in this book and invited me into their worlds: *Jacket2*, Extreme Text Folio, edited by Divya Victor; *BathHouse Journal*, Issue 18: Viscera, edited by Rosie Stockton; *Makhzin* and 98weeks, Issue 3: Dictationship, edited by Mirene Arsanios, Iman Mersal, and Ghalya Saadawi; *No Dear*, Issue 19: Republic, edited by Emily Brandt, Alex Cuff, and t'ai freedom ford; *Nat. Brut* Issue 17, edited by Meghan Lamb.

Thanks to my brilliant and generous first readers, especially Wayne Koestenbaum and Roberto Tejada, Lucy Lippard, Raquel Gutiérrez, Divya Victor, Sara Jane Stoner, Katherine Agard, Cyrus Stuvland, Ariel Yelen, Mei-mei Berssenbrugge, Anselm Berrigan, Renee Gladman, Anna Moschovakis, Marina Rosenfeld, Catherine Lord, Bill Dietz, Amber Musser, Amy Wan, Kendra Sullivan, and James Louis Stephens.

To the Poetry Project, NYC, my wholehearted appreciation for both invitations to read early drafts and an incredible site for poetry, with special gratitude for Laura Henriksen, Nicole Wallace, and Kyle Dacuyan.

To the Center for Contemporary Arts, Santa Fe, for the 2020 Living Room Series, with thanks to Amara Nash, Miriam

Sagan, and the poets who took a chance on shared thinking during a time of global crisis: Naima Yael Tokunow, mai c. doan, Jaye Elizabeth Elijah, Mallika Singh, Natalie Earnhart, Manny Loley, Boderra Joe, Emma Gomis, Stacy Szymaszek, and Rosie Stockton.

To the Decolonial Thought Reading Group, that supportive continuance of conversation and reading with Lou Cornum and Luke Church at the Graduate Center. With deep thanks as well to my doctoral cohort at the Graduate Center, especially Chy Sprauve, Anna Zeemont, Maxine Krenzel, and Shoumik Battacharya.

To my Bard MFA crew of co-conspirators Mirene Arsanios, Alex Cuff, Layli Long Soldier, Camonghne Felix, Mel Elberg, Barb Smith, Josh Escobar, Yasamin Ghiasi, and Hadi Fallahpisheh.

To NMPoetics, especially Genji Amino, with Maryam Parhizkar, Marina Eskeets, Daryl Lucero, Tori Cárdenas, Barbara Calderón-Douglass, Mat Galindo, Malinda Galindo, Ryan Dennison, Martha Tuttle, Avery Williamson, Autumn Chacon, Suzanne Kite, Szu-Han Ho, Edie Tsong, Valeria Tsygankova, Benny Lichtner, Jane Cope, Arthur Sze, Jennifer Denetdale, Dorothy Wang, Will Alexander, and Jane Lin.

To my family.

To Zach Valdez and Sara Deniz Akant, two individuals who showed me what friendship in art can be.

Finally, to Michelle Gurule who breathed fresh life into the pages of *The Kármán Line* and into me.